American Foreign Policy in Regions of Conflict

AMERICAN FOREIGN POLICY IN THE 21ST CENTURY

Edited by Thomas H. Henriksen

Published by Palgrave Macmillan:

American Foreign Policy in Regions of Conflict: A Global Perspective
By Howard J. Wiarda

America and the Rogue States
By Thomas H. Henriksen

American Foreign Policy in Regions of Conflict

A Global Perspective

Howard J. Wiarda

palgrave
macmillan

AMERICAN FOREIGN POLICY IN REGIONS OF CONFLICT
Copyright © Howard J. Wiarda, 2011.

First published in hardcover in 2011 by PALGRAVE MACMILLAN® in the United States—a division of St. Martin's Press LLC, 175 Fifth Avenue, New York, NY 10010.

Where this book is distributed in the UK, Europe and the rest of the world, this is by Palgrave Macmillan, a division of Macmillan Publishers Limited, registered in England, company number 785998, of Houndmills, Basingstoke, Hampshire RG21 6XS.

Palgrave Macmillan is the global academic imprint of the above companies and has companies and representatives throughout the world.

Palgrave® and Macmillan® are registered trademarks in the United States, the United Kingdom, Europe and other countries.

ISBN: 978–1–137–26688–0

The Library of Congress has cataloged the hardcover edition as follows:

Wiarda, Howard J., 1939–
      American foreign policy in regions of conflict : a global perspective / Howard J. Wiarda.
            p. cm.—(American foreign policy in the 21st century)
            ISBN 978–0–230–11502–6 (hardback)
          1. United States—Foreign relations—2009– 2. Conflict management—United States. I. Title.

JZ1480.W49 2011
327.73—dc22   2010048483

A catalogue record of the book is available from the British Library.

Design by Newgen Imaging Systems (P) Ltd., Chennai, India.

First PALGRAVE MACMILLAN paperback edition: September 2012

10 9 8 7 6 5 4 3 2 1

Printed in the United States of America.

Contents

Note from the Editor

America confronts an altered and still-unfolding international landscape since the collapse of the Soviet Union. For over four decades, the United States marshaled its military, economic, political, and ideological energies to contain and defeat the USSR. The disintegration of the Soviet nemesis in 1991 transformed international relations and American foreign policy. The momentous end of the bipolar stand-off has ushered in an increasingly complex, less safe, and more unpredictable world with start of the twenty-first century.

The United States now faces a broad range of challenges. Among the seemingly traditional international affairs, Washington contemplates the return of great power rivalries with an ascendant China, resurgent Russia, and self-reliant European Union. Rising regional powers, such as India, Iran, and Brazil, complicate the global picture in ways unimagined during the Cold War.

Additionally, there are important and troubled bilateral relations with Pakistan, Venezuela, North Korea, and Mexico, to cite a few countries that scarcely registered on the State Department's radar in the previous era. Prospects for a Middle East peace and a stable region appear more elusive than ever despite global changes, adding another dimension to the ongoing turbulence in Afghanistan and Iraq.

Our new era is also marked by new—or re-emerging—problems. Terrorism, piracy, ethnic conflicts, climate change, environmental degradation, nuclear proliferation, energy demands, economic globalization, and the role of international law on a host of issues—all (as well as other topics) beg to be addressed, navigated, or resolved.

This series recognizes that a page has turned in America's global role. It also takes into account that foreign policy cannot concentrate alone on state-to-state negotiations in isolation from the intricacies of other burgeoning concerns. It seeks to shed light on America's responses to the new reality. How the United States has responded—or should respond—to a wide variety of twenty-first century issues worldwide forms the central theme of the series.

THOMAS H. HENRIKSEN
Senior Fellow
Stanford University's Hoover Institution

Preface

I began my academic career in 1965 as a comparative politics scholar specializing in Latin America. Our goal, that of my contemporaries and myself, was to acquire specialized knowledge, or area studies expertise, in the Latin America region. That meant a thorough immersion in both political science *and* the history, geography, economics, sociology, languages, and culture of Latin America. And the assumption was that we would use our specialized academic knowledge to help enlighten and improve U.S. policy toward the area.

Foreign policy then, in those halcyon years of John F. Kennedy's New Frontier, Lyndon Johnson's Great Society, and such new and exciting foreign policy initiatives as the Peace Corps, the Alliance for Progress, and the Agency for International Development, would be based on a thorough, first-hand knowledge of the countries and areas affected. These were the years, the 1960s, of "the politics of the developing areas" and of a close connection between academia and policymaking, as we all struggled to understand the phenomenon of the new or emerging nations and their newfound importance on the world stage.

Policymaking in those years often looked to academia for knowledge and advice, while we in the academic world expected, perhaps naively, that our research findings would be widely read and used by policymakers. There was a close connection between *analyzing* development from an academic perspective *and* a policy of *bringing* development to less-favored countries. The assumption was that academic and specialized country or regional expertise would be used to inform public policy; sometimes we academic scholars had real policy influence.

But then, several large events transpired that made this close relationship between academia and policy strained and acrimonious:

1. The Vietnam War produced a sharp division between academics, especially those who studied Third World development, and the Johnson administration.
2. President Richard Nixon, suspicious that most academics were Democrats, cut many of the links and programs that had existed between academia and policymakers.
3. The rise and expansion of the Washington-based and savvy think tanks—the American Enterprise Institute (AEI), the Brookings Institution, the Center for Strategic and International Studies (CSIS), the Heritage Foundation, and other more specialized research cum policy groups—meant policy-relevant advice would come mainly from these institutions and no longer from the nation's universities.
4. Because of the ongoing Vietnam War, Watergate, and Nixon's disgrace, academia became more radical, more politicized, and cut off from policymaking.
5. Meanwhile, the field of political science, including its subfields of international relations and comparative politics, became more quantitative, mathematical, and "scientific," concerned more, like economics, with fashioning abstract mathematical modeling than proffering advice to policymakers.

By 1980, after having spent the first fifteen years of my career in academia, I was quite unhappy with the trends developing in political science and in academia more generally. During 1979–1981, I had retooled at Harvard University's prestigious Center for International Affairs (CFIA, now the Weatherhead Center) as a foreign policy specialist. And then in 1981 I was called to Washington to begin a twenty-plus-year stint in the think tank/policy spheres. I only returned full-time to academia in 2003 when I was offered an endowed chair in international relations and the headship of a brand new Department of International Affairs in a leading American university.

Going back to academia and to the field of international relations after a near-quarter-century-long absence was a bit of a shock. I do not wish to exaggerate the changes because much good and policy-relevant research and writing still goes on within the nation's universities. But the trends are clearly in some other directions and we need to know what those are. First, the field of international relations, like political science more generally, has become much more "scientific," to the exclusion of more qualitative and interpretive points of view. Second, in its emphasis on rational choice, mathematical modeling, and research methodology for its own sake, the field has largely abandoned the older idea of informing policy. Third, culture, history, geography, and language and area studies have all been denigrated in favor of developing measurable "data sets," often of dubious scientific merit. And fourth, the interconnections between the policy worlds and academia have been definitively cut, with the two proceeding in quite different directions and having few, if any, connections between them.

I believe these trends are dangerous and fundamentally wrong, and that is what this book is all about. I want to see the links between academic research in political science and international relations *and* the world of policymaking restored. Second, I want a place in political science, IR, and comparative politics research for policy-relevant research. Third, I believe such factors as history, geography, political culture, and area studies should be restored to their rightful place in political science research. And fourth, I want to see these factors incorporated into our considerations of U.S. policy in distinct areas of the world.

Increasingly, I have found in Washington foreign policy-making many of the same trends that have been occurring in academic international relations research. These trends, reflecting the mammoth increase in the data available through spy satellites, sophisticated listening devices, and so on, are much more pronounced in the CIA, the National Security Agency, and the Department of Defense than they are in the State Department—although their general direction is apparent throughout foreign policy-making. That is, the use of mathematical modeling to the exclusion of more interpretive methods; the employment of quantitative methods that exclude such factors as geography, culture, and history; and the lack of appreciation for the necessity of thorough area, country, and language expertise in interpreting the data. I am convinced these trends help explain why U.S. policy so often goes astray in so many parts of the world: we don't *know* or speak the languages of the countries and areas we are dealing with (witness Iraq or Afghanistan).

And that is the second main theme of the book. While political science and its subfield international relations are seeking to become more quantitative and "scientific," the world and its 190-odd political systems keep on changing. And our substantive knowledge of them, both of individual countries and regions *and* the shifting patterns among them, becomes less and less. That is particularly so at the policy level where there is a sharp disconnect between knowledge (or better, the lack thereof) of countries and regions *and* enlightened policy. Here is where the field of comparative politics comes in, for comparative politics, with its focus on countries, geographic culture areas, and global trends, can help enlighten international relations and foreign policy.

That is what this book seeks to do. Its essential theoretical contribution is to reintegrate the field of comparative politics back into international relations and foreign policy studies. It does so by a thorough knowledge of and first-hand experience in all the countries and areas covered. Which is to say, it reintroduces local and regional history, geography, culture studies, language, and informed interpretation back into foreign policy considerations. Essentially, we are saying, you need to know the countries and areas with which you're dealing before you can have good, informed, enlightened policy toward them. The point seems obvious but it is not, either in academia or, increasingly, in policymaking. Witness the imbroglios and policy confusion in which we have found ourselves, earlier in Vietnam and now in Iraq, Pakistan, Afghanistan, Iran, North Korea, Somalia, and other embattled places.

Following an introduction that spells out in more detail the themes of this introduction, making the case for comparative politics and area studies to inform foreign policy decision-making, we proceed to a discussion of all the major regional areas: Europe East and West, Russia, Asia, the Middle East, Latin America, and Africa. Each chapter is informed by a thorough understanding of the area, its development, and its dynamics, before we get into the discussion of U.S. foreign policy toward that area. Moreover, in each chapter we use a common outline, both to organize better our thinking about each area *and* to emphasize that first we need to thoroughly comprehend each area *before* we can make informed policy recommendations about it. The book has an area or regional focus, we might add, but where the discussion requires further elaboration in terms of treatment of individual countries—for example, France, Germany, and Great Britain in Europe; Japan, China, and India in Asia; Brazil and Mexico in Latin America—we provide that as well.

The result, I believe, is a book that is knowledgeable and well-informed about the countries and areas with which we deal, *and* that makes recommendations for policy based on this informed view. That is how policy *should* be made, I'm sure all of us will agree, but in a surprising number of cases is not. I should say that this volume on "Regions of Conflict" serves as a complement to my earlier foreign policy book that focuses on the *domestic* basis of U.S. foreign policymaking.[1] For policy to be successful, we must know and understand both the countries and regions of the world affected, *and* the process by which policy is made domestically in the United States.

Let me illustrate these points by reference to one of the most significant of recent events, the so-called "Arab Spring." In rapid succession longtime dictators in Tunisia, Egypt, Libya, and Yemen fell, often assisted or pushed by the United States. Foreign policy was driven by the promise of democracy, but so far none of these countries has become democratic. Getting rid of a dictator is far easier than building democracy, which may take two or three generations, not years. It's almost impossible to create democracy in these countries in the almost complete absence of civil society, democratic institutions, or a political culture supportive of democracy. Had US foreign policy been grounded in a thorough understanding of the culture, society, politics, and low socio-economic development of these countries, as well as Iraq and Afghanistan foreign policy might not have stumbled as badly as it did. In short, international relations and foreign policy need to be deeply grounded and informed by a deep understanding of the countries and regions with which we deal.

This book would not have been possible without the support of numerous institutions and individuals over the years. My understanding of Washington policymaking has been enhanced by my three decades of living in the nation's capital and my work there at AEI, the

State Department, Georgetown and George Washington Universities, CSIS, the National War College and the Defense Department, and the Woodrow Wilson International Center for Scholars. My writings are also informed by frequent travel and research in *all* the areas discussed, and by regular participation in the forums and discussions along the Washington policy circuit: the Carnegie Endowment, Brookings, the Council on Foreign Relations, the Atlantic Council, the Hudson Institute, the Potomac Institute, and numerous others of the Washington policy shops. These forums not only add to your knowledge base but also sharpen your analytic skills as you weigh different policy options.

The School of Public and International Affairs (SPIA) at the University of Georgia and its dean Thomas P. Lauth have been especially generous with their leave policy and research support, enabling me to travel widely, carry out the research, and spend time in the writing of this work. My colleagues in the Department of International Affairs have been, all at once, commentators, critics, and, occasionally, foils for my strong views about foreign policy and international relations. Annie Kryzanek continues to serve as my indispensable research assistant, Doris Holden did yeoman service as usual in typing the manuscript, and Kathryn Johnson shepherded it to the publisher. But my greatest debt, as always, goes to my wife Iêda, another political scientist in the family, without whose support and patience this book and others earlier would not have been possible. Of course, I alone am responsible for any mistakes of fact or interpretation that remain in the book.

HOWARD J. WIARDA
Washington, D.C.
Winter 2011

Note

1. Howard J. Wiarda, *Divided America on the World Stage: Broken Government and Foreign Policy* (Washington, D.C.: Potomac Publishers, 2009).

CHAPTER 1

Introduction

International relations (IR) today is a very different field from what it was forty and fifty years ago. The research is much more specialized and empirical and has little to do with actual foreign policy-making. It seeks to build mathematical models that are, presumably, universally applicable. Based on a few simple assumptions, the IR field is now closer to economics, with its assumptions of the rational, calculating, self-interested, and self-maximizing individual, a notion that is similarly—or at least most economists believe—universally applicable. The field of international relations, in short, has become "scientific." And in the process, those who teach the more traditional foreign policy courses, which are of more interest to most students, have become increasingly marginalized within their own departments and universities.

The study of international relations has, in addition, become more and more separated from the *practice* of foreign policy. As international relations has become more "scientific" in its aspirations, foreign policy practitioners have come to rely on it less and less. There is a real problem here: increasingly, American foreign policy relies less and less on a thorough knowledge and understanding of other countries, areas, and worldwide trends. The link between academic scholarship and foreign policy has been broken. The aim, not modest, of this book is to reverse that trend: to show the continued relevance of a deep knowledge of the world's political systems to a better and more informed foreign policy. Our goal is to reintegrate the fields of comparative politics and international relations back into the work and thinking of foreign policy practitioners.

International Relations and Foreign Policy

International relations and comparative politics were the two fields within political science that had longest and most strenuously resisted the newer, more scientific orientation of the discipline. The "behavioral" or "scientific" revolution in political science began in the 1950s; for a long time it was confined to the subfield of American politics (political parties, electoral behavior, and voting analysis) within political science. International relations and comparative politics, whose domains covered the whole world and all of the globe's now 190-odd countries, were thought to be too varied and too diverse culturally to be encompassed in one single methodology and approach. The assumption was, which was widely accepted if often lamented, that the cultural differences among distinct global areas were so great as to rule out much theory and model building on a universal basis.[1]

The situation in the comparative politics field was very similar to that of IR. That is, it was based on careful study and analysis but the methodology was mainly interpretive rather than scientific. The approach was systematic and analytic but, given the vast cultural differences between nations and geographic regions, few scholars attempted to do quantitative studies. This is because even if you could get accurate polling or voting data (most often a doubtful prospect), for example, the voting act itself often has a different philosophical basis in different countries, involving real choice in some but a plebiscitary or a ratification act in others. Hence, most scholars in the 1960s and 1970s approached comparative politics from the point of view of seeking to comprehend and understand foreign countries and cultures in which they developed expertise. And for many in the comparative field, such knowledge and understanding were for the purpose of helping American foreign policy to better understand other countries, and thus improve the policy.[2]

Today, international relations is much more heavily engaged in the search for quantification. It aspires to be more rigorous and empirical. Interpretation is out while mathematical modeling is in. Analysis based on cultural and regional differences are also out while models that presume to analyze universal trends are in. In the process of these changes, the older close connection between research work and policy recommendations is being lost.

Increasingly, IR uses the methods of game theory, rational choice, and mathematical decision making. Those are all useful techniques. The question remains whether these methodologies have importance in themselves, as many in the field now think, or whether they are merely a means to an end—the "end" being a better understanding of other countries or of policy. In other words, is the tail (methodology) now wagging the dog (policy substance)? The new division within the field seems to be between those who use the newer methodologies but consider them only a tool of research aimed at helping to inform policy, and those for whom the methodology has become the main subject matter while policy recommendations are relegated to the sidelines or considered a purely private political matter quite independent of one's research.

With this new "scientific" orientation in IR and comparative politics, such elements as history, culture, religion, geography, and environment no longer count. They are dismissed as irrelevant. Why? First, because under globalization, all persons will presumably want the same things—democracy, civil society, and a mixed private-public economy. Or, as the slogan of the 1990s put it, with the Soviet Union having collapsed and authoritarianism discredited, democracy was "the only game in town." But that is a position that ignores that democracy is not the only game in China, Russia, Iran, North Korea, Cuba, Myanmar, and numerous other countries. Or that democracy may take, in distinct countries, a great variety of, in part, culturally derived forms.

And second, because the models these more scientifically oriented approaches use presume universal relevance and applicability. If they are universally relevant, then, presumably, factors such as geography, history, culture, or region have no validity. But that is surely an indefensible position. We know that, for example, the *geographic* proximity of Eastern Europe to Western Europe helped to consolidate Eastern European democracy; we know that the fact the Czech Republic had a *history* of democracy before World War II also helped it *re*establish democracy after the Iron Curtain fell. We know that *culture* has an effect on the limited democratic progress in the Islamic

Middle East; we also know that, *regionally*, when one or several countries in a region democratize, it becomes easier for others to do so. It
is ludicrous for scholars to dismiss as irrelevant factors that are so self-
evidently important; surely some greater modesty in the advancement
of those models that claim global applicability is called for.

One understands the logic of this more "scientific" approach. If you
truly believe, like economics, that your data sets and methodology are
globally applicable, that your model is independent of culture, history, geography, and background, then there is no need to study other
distinct cultures, languages, religions, or sociologies. One model fits
all! Regardless of different cultures and customs, you employ a global,
cookie-cutter approach that uses a single mold for all countries. But
that approach is what got us in so much trouble first in Vietnam and
now in Iran, Afghanistan, and Pakistan. Note how even the best of
our commanders, despite now having anthropologists and historians
embedded in their units, are seeking to apply what "worked" in Iraq
to the situation in Afghanistan, a country that culturally, politically,
economically, and sociologically is so much different from Iraq. Can
it work? I doubt it.

A single model, as in economics, that presumes to explain human
behavior on a worldwide basis is undoubtedly attractive. It strains cre-
dulity, however, to think that all of human behavior, in all its rich
variety and multiculturalism, can be reduced to a single behavioral
model.

The field of comparative politics has been less affected by the "scientific" approach, or what has recently come to be called the "rational
choice" approach, than others. Comparativists have tended to think
the world is too culturally diverse and too complex for any one single
model of political behavior to apply. Distinct areas and countries think
differently, have different priorities, and see and understand things in
different ways. How can all of human behavior, in all its diverse and
multicultural dimensions, be subsumed to one rather simple, single-
causal explanation? The answer, comparativists have historically said,
is that it can't, and that is the purpose of comparative politics: to
compare both similarities *and differences* among nations.

Do not get us wrong here. We are all in favor of a more vigorous, more scientific comparative politics, *where that is appropriate*.
Heretofore, for example, the approaches of game theory and rational

choice have been largely applied in the research areas of political party competition, legislative voting, and elections behavior—all research that applies mainly in stable, developed, democratic states. But what of those many of us who study developing nations, where elections may be but one route to power among several. Actually, I see no reason why the methodology of rational choice cannot with equal validity be applied in the developing areas to such phenomena as revolutions, general strikes, and coups d'état. Our difference with the rational choice approach is not its usefulness in the right circumstances, but its elevation from a single if useful explanation to a total and all-encompassing one. The political world is not nearly so simple that it can all be crammed into one single methodology.

It was intellectual gadfly William Buckley who made famous the quip that academic disputes, usually over methodology, are so nasty because the stakes are so low. In the argument we have been making here, the stakes are very high: the future of American foreign policy. At this stage we need to put on our Washington think-tank and policy hats, as distinct from the academic one. For in Washington, where the foreign policy stakes are high (Iran, Iraq, Afghanistan, Pakistan, North Korea, Arab-Israeli relations), the problem is a growing one, and often with life-and-death, real-world consequences. For in Washington as well as the nation's universities, we have numerous policymakers who are well trained in international relations. They know all the pros and cons of realist, neorealist, and liberal internationalist models of IR. But they too often know no foreign languages, have never lived abroad (as distinct from brief travels), and fail to understand other cultures in their own, distinct, nonethnocentric terms.

No wonder policy so often goes astray not only in the key countries listed earlier but also in Haiti, Somalia, Yemen, and others too numerous to mention. So can we ever understand and come to grips with non-Western cultures and have enlightened policies toward the Third World? First, our language training, culture training, and foreign area studies are wholly inadequate: we do not, by and large, study or speak foreign languages, and if we study foreign cultures at all, it is mostly from the point of view of why they can't be just like us. And second, in the academic realms, to admit to the importance of language training and area studies would be to admit that all those sophisticated global models mentioned earlier may not be universally valid after all.

There may be hope yet. Among the entering classes in many graduate programs, the students are split about fifty-fifty between those who want a policy career and thus take history, culture, geography, and local environmental factors seriously, and those who want what I call a "political sciency" or academic career and thus go into mathematical modeling. The faculty, of course, compete to lure the students into the two respective camps. Meanwhile, in many universities, new master's program in international policy (MIP) for students more interested in a foreign policy career have been introduced, to go along with the traditional MA and PhD degrees for those more interested in a university teaching or academic career. Occasionally, in fact, these two career tracks even meet.

Empathy, Understanding, and Foreign Policy

The world is a very different place than it was twenty years ago, at the end of the Cold War. And because the world has been changed in fundamental ways, U.S. foreign policy needs to be changed in fundamental ways as well.

Among the changes of the last two decades are the following:

- The Soviet Union, our historic Cold War enemy, has collapsed; the successor state, Russia, is much weaker and less of a threat than the old USSR.
- Western Europe and its individual countries have become less important in U.S. strategic thinking. Once the Cold War ended, Europe was no longer seen as a superpower battlefield; U.S attention is now concentrated elsewhere and Europe is staking out its own foreign policy directions independent of the United States.
- Eastern Europe, once under Soviet control, has become free, democratic, with a modern mixed economy, and integrated into the European Union (EU) and the North Atlantic Treaty Organization (NATO). In some ways, we are more closely allied with the countries of Eastern Europe than with Western Europe.
- East Asia has become much wealthier and more important; quite a number of Asian countries—Japan, South Korea, China, India—are major actors on the world scene. Power in the world arena is clearly shifting to Asia.

- China, especially, has become a powerhouse, the world's second largest (after the United States, ahead of Japan and Germany) economy, an emerging global power, and perhaps a future super-power challenger of the United States.
- The Middle East, with its oil, strategic importance, terrorism, wealth, and now the potential for nuclear weapons in Iran and elsewhere, has become much more important in U.S. foreign policy thinking.
- The United States is more interdependent with Latin America on a greater variety of issues—immigration, trade, terrorism, drugs, labor supplies, oil, natural gas, borders, crime, and so on—than any other world area. Yet we have never developed a consistent, mature policy for dealing with Latin America. Argentina, Brazil, Chile, Mexico are all of rising importance.
- Africa is similarly of rising importance: the potential for terrorism, AIDS, wealth from vast mineral and natural resources, domestic politics, increased competition from China and India. The Department of Defense has created AFRICOM to deal with Africa's rising important; now it is up to the public and the rest of the U.S. government to update its thinking on Africa.

Here, then, we have a clear and extremely provocative hypothesis to begin our discussion. The continents and world areas that are the subject of this book truly are "adrift." By our preliminary analysis, two regions and/or countries are of declining importance to U.S policy: Russia and Western Europe. By contrast, four global regions—Asia, the Middle East, Latin America, and Africa—are of rising importance on the United States' list of priorities. Moreover, of these areas of rising importance, the United States pays serious attention and has a serious policy toward only two of them: East Asia and the Middle East. For the most part it treats the other two- Latin America and Africa—with indifference and what is often termed "benign neglect," which often turns out to be not so benign. Not only are the continents adrift in terms of their changing importance, U.S. policy is adrift, uncertain, and ill-defined in quite a few areas of the world as well.

According to the "realist" school of international relations, the United States should, in dealing with these global areas, be concerned only with its own national interests. Well, of course, that is true on a very superficial level: all countries including the United States seek to pursue their own national interests.

But that is not the issue. The real question is: in seeking to pursue our national interest, do we follow an enlightened version of our self-interests or an unenlightened one. Most of us prefer the former over the latter.

My colleagues and I come out of a comparative politics background in political science. That means that we study other countries and regions of the world. To use the technical definition for a minute, we are dedicated to the comparative and systematic study of other countries and regions. We look for trends, patterns, and regularities among nations. We analyze both similarities and differences. How and why do some countries develop and others not? Why do some countries become failed states? Why do some countries rise in power (China, India, Brazil) and others (Great Britain, France, Russia) decline? Those questions are at the heart of what students of comparative politics explore. A moment's reflection will indicate that the answers to these questions are also essential to foreign policy. For policy needs to know how, why, and when countries rise in power, when they decline, when they fail. Such knowledge is essential to a successful foreign policy.

One of the things that comparative politics teaches is the need for empathy and understanding in studying other counties and "culture areas"—areas of the world such as East Asia, the Middle East, Latin America, or Sub-Saharan Africa where there are common currents of culture and society. Empathy means that you study and comprehend other countries and culture areas on their own terms, through their own eyes, and in their own language or languages. This is hard to do and requires long years of work, because our natural inclination is to look at other countries through our own lenses. But that will not do: you can't look at the rest of the world through your own cultural binoculars and prejudices and expect to understand it. That is called "ethnocentrism"—putting your own cultural, ethnic, or national perspective first, to the exclusion of other peoples' or countries' points of view—and is the opposite of empathy.

Utilizing empathy in understanding other countries does not mean you have to put aside your own cultural values entirely. We are not here advocating cultural relativism—the motion that all cultures and all political systems are of equal value and therefore we must not condemn them and draw our own moral conclusions. I have personally decided, for example, that I do not like the Iranian regime of the mullahs and Islamic fundamentalism. But as a scholar, or as a diplomat, to understand and deal with that regime I would certainly want to know the language, visit there, talk to the people, find out what they're thinking, and so on. I would also have some empathy with Iran's desire to develop as a nation, to rediscover its Persian heritage, and to assert its independence. All that requires empathy. But empathy would not keep me from condemning that regime for its widespread human rights violations, its treatment of women, or its repression. The moral should be, "When in Rome (or Tehran), do as the Romans (or Iranians) do"—to the point where it offends your own moral sensibility.

Having a good and effective foreign policy requires a deep understanding of the countries or regions you are dealing with. And that requires traveling there, living there, learning the languages, steeping yourself in the country's culture, understanding its goals and aspirations, truly understanding the country from the inside, from an empathetic viewpoint. If you are a scholar, that means lengthy periods of field research in your country or region of specialization; if you are a policymaker, that means an assignment in the country before you start making policy decisions. Sitting in your faculty office back in the United States if you are a scholar or skipping the language and orientation course at the Foreign Service Institute if you are a State Department official is not a good way to acquire expertise on your country.

Good policy can only be based on a thorough, empathetic understanding of the country or countries you must deal with. Good policy must also be based on mutual interest. Each "party" or country must get something out of the deal or agreement if it is to work and produce beneficial results. The United States, since it is a superpower, can be arrogant and sometimes *impose* its favored solutions on other, weaker countries. But such impositions of U.S.-preferred solutions will not work in the long run. Nor will it work, as President George W. Bush suggested to other countries after the terrorist attacks of 9/11, that "You're either for us or against us." That's too simple. The world doesn't work that way. It's mutual interests—the other country's and your own—that need to be served, not just the needs or interests of one partner in the relationship.

The field of comparative politics in political science is uniquely qualified to provide such a perspective. For comparative politics seeks analytically and systematically to understand other countries and regions—and to do so empathetically and on their own terms. Through such understanding of foreign countries, the field of comparative politics has a lot to say to the field of international relations. For if we want to have good relations and serve the mutual interests of our own and other counties, we need that level of empathetic understanding. In this way, comparative politics can also help our diplomacy and political leadership by shedding light and in-depth knowledge of other countries where we have important relations. Government officials often have limited time or opportunity to acquire such knowledge; comparatively politics can usefully fill in where there are voids in our knowledge.

The Book: A Look Ahead

In subsequent chapters, we review U.S. policy toward all the key regions of the world: Europe East and West, Russia, Asia, the Middle East, Latin America, and Africa. Canada and Australia/New Zealand are left out, not because they are unimportant but because U.S. relations with these countries are generally peaceful and more or less harmonious, and in this book we want particularly to focus on regions of conflict.

In this book we seek to understand these countries and regions in terms of *their own* history, culture, geography, and background. We seek to understand them in their own settings, languages, and aspirations rather than through the lenses of our own, American, rose-colored glasses. The approach is deliberately nonethnocentric, on the assumption that American policy works best if we can *harmonize* our relations with other countries' needs, interests, and aspirations rather than America seeking to *impose* solutions on the rest of the world. The best diplomacy, we have found, is when we are able to find grounds of *common* interest and understanding and resolve issues in ways that *all* the parties benefit from, when *mutual* interests are served, and *not just* those of the United States alone.

The approach in each chapter is thus to begin with a discussion of why that particular country or region is important in its own right and, therefore, to the United States. The second section of each chapter focuses on the social, economic, political, and cultural background of that country or area. We seek here to understand them rather than to preach to them, missionary style. In other words, in this section we build the approach of comparative politics back into the study of international relations. Only in the third section of each chapter do we begin to discuss U.S. policy and interests in the country/region under review and whether these can be made to correspond to the interests and aspirations of the country affected. Next we analyze problem areas, conflicts, and ongoing issues that may still be at variance. A final section offers conclusions and recommendations and, if needed, analyzes U.S. relations with specific countries within these distinct regions.

The result is a unique book in the international relations/foreign policy field. It brings back, gone for a time in academia, the close relations between comparative politics and foreign policy. It argues forcefully that you cannot have good relations (IR) with a country or area unless you first understand it—and on its own terms and in its own language(s) and culture, which only comparative politics can provide. It advances an empathetic view of other countries' goals and aspirations and seeks to set U.S. policy on a course, for the most part, in harmony with these. Of course, it recognizes that there are some countries/regions where our relations will still be difficult, complex, and maybe even conflictual. But to the extent possible, it seeks to recast American foreign policy in ways that enable us to identify with other countries' needs, aims. and even complexes rather than be in conflict with them. In short, it advances a positive and an opportunity-based foreign policy instead of one that so often historically has been negative and threat-based.

Notes

1. Howard J. Wiarda, *Divided America on the World Stage: Broken Government and Foreign Policy* (Washington, D.C.: Potomac Publishers, 2009).
2. Among members of this earlier generation, there were two main motivations for studying political science professionally: because of intrinsic

interest in the subject matter *and* to contribute to better policy. Among today's generation of political scientists, however, this second purpose, while not explicitly repudiated, is in decline.

Suggested Readings

Berger, Peter and Samuel P Huntington (eds.). *Many Globalizations* (New York: Oxford University Press, 1995).

Diamond, Larry. *Developing Democracy* (Baltimore: John Hopkins University Press, 1999).

Dogan, Mattei and Dominique Pelassy. *How to Compare Nations* (Chatham, NJ: Chatham House, 1984).

Fukuyama, Francis. *The End of History and the Last Man* (New York: Macmillan, 1992).

Horowitz, Irving L. *Three Worlds of Development* (New York: Oxford University Press, 1972).

Huntington, Samuel P. *The Clash of Civilizations and the Remakings of World Order* (New York: Simon and Schuster, 1996).

———. *The Third Wave: Democratization in the Late Twentieth Century* (Norman, OK: University of Oklahoma Press, 1991).

Kaplan, Robert. *The Coming Anarchy: Shattering the Dreams of the Post-Cold War* (New York: Vintage, 2000).

Lake, Anthony et al. *Our Worst Enemy: The Unmaking of American Foreign Policy* (New York: Simon and Schuster, 1984).

Nye, Joseph and John D. Donahue (eds.). *Governance in Globalizing World* (Washington, D.C.: Brookings Institution, 2000).

Wiarda, Howard J. *Divided America on the World Stage: Broken Government and Foreign Policy* (Washington, D.C.: Potomac Publishers, 2009).

———. (ed.). *U.S. Foreign and Strategic Policy in the Post-Cold War Era* (Westport, CT: Greenwood Press, 1996).

CHAPTER 2

Western Europe

Western Europe is one of the world's most developed and sophisticated areas. It often likes to think of itself as *the* most modern and progressive region, ahead of the United States in social programs, humanitarianism, and lifestyle, if not in military might. And therein lies an initial problem: Europe is sometimes a bit arrogant in claiming to be more advanced than the United States, while the Europeans at the same time often say that it is the United States that acts arrogantly in world affairs. Is there enough blame in these claims and counterclaims for both sides of the Atlantic to feel vindicated?

Historically, at least since the sixteenth century, Europe has been *the* center of world politics. And, for most of the twentieth century, America's strongest allies, as well as its largest conflicts, have been in Europe. From America's point of view, it came to the defense of and literally "saved" Europe (from itself?) in the twentieth century's greatest conflicts: World War I, World War II, and the Cold War with the Soviet Union and its Warsaw Pact (Eastern European) allies. Europe does not necessarily dispute this reading of history, but it believes we are now in a new era with new issues and that we must adapt our foreign policy accordingly. The United States, Europe argues, has not kept pace with the new conditions.

Much of our culture in America, our political traditions and institutions, our language, our legal system, our educational institutions, our economy, and our dominant immigrant communities came, historically, from Europe. Specifically from northern (Great Britain, the Netherlands, Germany), Protestant, what Samuel P. Huntington calls "Anglo-Protestant" Europe initially,[1] and then in the late nineteenth and early twentieth centuries increasingly from Southern and Eastern and Catholic Europe. Now, with strong immigration coming from Asia, Latin America and the Caribbean, the Middle East, and sub-Saharan Africa, and with the United States becoming more diverse and multicultural, the question of whether we are still an Anglo-Protestant and, therefore, a "European" country is more and more contested. Certainly, in our immigration laws we do not and cannot say that we favor Europeans (a code word for "whites") over others.

While the United States and Western Europe, because of our common history and culture, the North Atlantic Treaty Organization (NATO), and the Trans-Atlantic Alliance, have been close in the past, now that ground is shifting. The United States and Western Europe are pulling apart. We are no longer as close as we once were. The reasons for this are various:

1. The end of the Cold War deprived us of our common enemy and purpose, containing the Soviet Union, and revealed fissures in the alliance that had not been perceived earlier.
2. The United States and Western Europe have drifted apart culturally, religiously, politically, economically, and in our respective views of the world. The common basis of understanding between us has eroded. More on this theme follows.
3. The generations have shifted; the old World War II/Cold War generation in America, now fading in influence, felt close to Europe, while the new generation in power (such as President Barack Obama) is more Third World (Africa, Asia, Latin America, the Middle East) oriented.
4. Our foreign policy priorities have shifted. It used to be, during most of the twentieth century, that Europe was our number one priority; now Asia, with its dynamic economies (Japan, China, India, South Korea, Taiwan, Hong Kong, Singapore), is at that position.

In this chapter we trace the evolution of U.S. policy toward Western Europe and explore how and why we are drifting apart. Nowadays, in terms of foreign and strategic policies, we seem at times to be closer to Eastern Europe (discussed in chapter three) than to Western Europe. Among the questions we ask here is whether the Trans-Atlantic Alliance can be resuscitated or are we now too far apart? Is the main political and military instrument of that alliance, NATO, worth renewing or, since the main purpose of NATO (containing and defeating the Soviet Union) has been accomplished, should we disband it? And should Europe be restored to its past number one priority or do the new global realities dictate that East Asia or the Middle East (Iraq, Iran, Afghanistan, Pakistan, the Israeli-Palestinian conflict) are now our top priorities?

U.S. relations with Europe are still important—some would say preeminently important—but they are of a special kind. Let us try to specify what makes them special:

1. In the United States, Canada (a member of NATO and of the Trans-Atlantic Alliance), and Western Europe, we are dealing exclusively with developed, modern states. There are *no* Third World countries here or the issues and problems that go with them. Note that in table 2.1 *all* the countries are in the high-income category.

2. The differences we have with the countries of Western Europe are, mainly, arguments among friends and allies. We have our disagreements to be sure, but no one in the Alliance is about to go to war with any other member.

3. The key issue for the United States in dealing with Western Europe is how much emphasis to give to this area. Is Europe still number one in U.S. priorities or has the U.S. emphasis now shifted to Asia, the Middle East, or Latin America?

4. The main topics of conversation between the United States and its European allies are what we will call "policing-the-world" issues, that is, what is, or should be, the allied response to bloody Bosnia and Kosovo in the former Yugoslavia, toward such unstable, possible terrorist sanctuaries as Iraq and Afghanistan, and toward a restored and newly aggressive Russia?

Table 2.1 Per capita income

Country	Per capita income (in $)	Income category
Austria	38,090	High income
Belgium	35,110	High income
Denmark	36,740	High income
Finland	35,270	High income
France	33,470	High income
Germany	33,820	High income
Greece	32,520	High income
Ireland	37,040	High income
Italy	29,900	High income
Luxembourg	64,400	High income
Netherlands	39,500	High income
Norway	53,690	High income
Portugal	20,640	High income
Spain	30,110	High income
Sweden	35,840	High income
Switzerland	43,080	High income
United Kingdom	34,370	High income
United States (for comparison)	45,850	High income

Source: World Bank, World Development Indicators, 2009.

Background

Western Europe has some of the richest countries and the highest standards of living—along with North America (the United States, Canada) and Japan and the "Four Tigers" (South Korea, Taiwan, Hong Kong, Singapore) in the world. *Every one* of the Western European countries makes the list of what the World Bank calls "high-income" countries. In Western Europe, literacy is almost universal; health standards and longevity are high; and there is very little poverty (see table 2.1).

Currently, the richest country in the world is Luxembourg, with a per capita income of $64,400. That is about two hundred times richer than the poor countries of the world. It is not that small Luxembourg has more resources or talents than other countries; it's that Luxembourg lies between also-rich France, Belgium, and

Germany and many wealthy members of these societies put their money in Luxembourg banks, which jacks up the national average. Luxembourg is thus an anomaly: a *super*-rich country within a region of similarly rich nations.

The second richest nation in the world is Norway at an average per person income of $53,690. Norway is a very highly developed country, but its big boost into the very top ranks of prosperity came with the discovery of rich, offshore, North Sea oil and natural gas deposits in the 1970s. Third richest is Switzerland ($43,080) with a diverse economy and sophisticated banking, followed by the Netherlands ($39,500), a wealthy commercial and trading nation. In short order, Austria, Belgium, Denmark, Finland, France, Germany, Iceland, Ireland, Sweden, and the United Kingdom follow—all in the mid-to-upper $30,000 per person range. Southern Europe—Greece, Italy, Portugal, and Spain—is somewhat poorer on average and with still existing pockets of poverty, but nevertheless still in the "high-income" category. Eastern Europe is considerably poorer; for that and its history and geostrategic position, it receives treatment in a separate chapter.

In addition to having a high per capita income, all these countries have a high life expectancy (higher than the United States), virtually no illiteracy, good health care, and a high standard of living. All of them are what we call "welfare states," although the level and degree of such services vary considerably. Great Britain, the Netherlands, and Germany are still on the more capitalistic side of the equation, while the Scandinavian countries of Denmark, Norway, and Sweden are on the more socialized side. The way we measure this is by the percentage of gross national product generated by the state, as opposed to the private sector: 40–50 percent in the more capitalistic countries, 60–80 percent in the more socialist-leaning ones. Thus, while all of these countries have "mixed" private-public economies, the degree or percentage of this mix may vary quite a lot.

Most of the European states have chosen to become social, social welfare, or social-democratic states. A larger share of the economy goes into the public sector than has been the case historically in the United States. That helps explain why, when Americans travel to Europe, they are amazed at the clean streets, the good public transportation systems, and public services in general. The reason for this is clear: Europeans are willing to pay for them in the form of high taxes (40–60 percent depending on the country), whereas in the United States the electorate has long preferred greater private disposable income and less money given up in taxes (about 30 percent) for public programs. But now under George W. Bush and Barack Obama the American tax burden has similarly risen to 40 percent, about the same level as Great Britain, Germany, or the Netherlands; the question is whether we will also, like the Europeans, get more back in the way of public services.

From this, it should be plain by now that, in the case of Western Europe, we're dealing with modern, developed nations and not underdeveloped or developing ones. These are all highly literate, well-educated, sophisticated countries at or about the same level as, and in some areas exceeding, the United States. These facts importantly shape our foreign relations. In none of these countries is instability, threats to democracy, regime change, or human rights abuses likely to be an issue. Particular *governments* may change but not, as in Iraq or Iran, entire *regimes*. Nor in Western Europe do we need to be concerned about civil war or armed insurrection or having to deal with extremist regimes of either the far left or the far right. AIDS epidemics, genocide, and armed conflicts between the countries are also pretty well ruled out. In other words, as countries climb the ladder of national development and become modern states, the nature of the *internal* issues they face, their *foreign* policies, and the nature of their relations with the United States all undergo fundamental transformations.

In Western Europe the issues we face and the nature of U.S.-European relations are not uncomplicated, but they are of a different kind and sort from those faced by the United States in other areas. With Western Europe there are many common traditions and understandings (although that, as we see later, is now also changing); in addition, the Western European nations and the United States are, ostensibly, allies through NATO and other agreements. So the main U.S. issues in this part of the world include how best to coordinate with our Western allies; how to arrive at a common policy in such hotspots as Iraq, Iran, Israeli-Palestinian relations, or Russia; whether to employ multilateral or bilateral strategies; "burden-sharing" (how much each country should contribute, in money or manpower, to the common defense); or what should be done about such out-of-area conflicts as Afghanistan, the Sudan, and genocide in its province of Darfur, or the admission of such countries as Belarus, Georgia, Turkey, and the Ukraine to NATO and/or to that other great institution of European unity (of which the United States is *not* a member), the European Union or EU. These are hard and fundamental issues among (mainly) allies and countries with common purposes, but they are not necessarily vital, life-and-death, or state-making or destroying issues as is the case with many Third World regimes.

Having said all this, it is important to emphasize as well that there are severe splits in the NATO alliance and, in general, between the United States and its historic European allies. On a *host* of issues the United States and the European countries are drifting farther apart. Our histories are different; our political cultures are different; our values and beliefs are different. There is no longer, especially absent the Cold War enemy the Soviet Union, a commodity of interests and understandings between us. As my colleague Robert Kagan has written, after having lived in Europe for a time, the United States is "from Mars" while Europe is "from Venus."[2] Let us explore what these increasing differences are.

U.S. Interests and Policy

The United States and Western Europe have very different attitudes and policies toward the world. At least two major factors are at work here: Europe's different geostrategic position from that of the United States, *and* the increasingly wide disparity between the political cultures of the two areas.

With regard to cultural and sociopolitical issues, the following factors help explain why Europe sees the world differently from the United States.

- It is estimated that 80 percent of Americans believe in God, while only 40 percent of Europeans do. About 50 percent of Americans attend church regularly, whereas less than 5 percent of Europeans do. Western Europe is much more secular than is the United States.
- Europeans tend to believe in a strong state, while Americans historically have been skeptical of a strong central government.

- Americans tend to be individualistic and competitive; Europeans are more oriented toward a collectivist and cooperative mentality.
- Europeans are proud of their advanced, state-run, social welfare systems, while Americans (until Obama?) have generally favored more private sector-dominated solutions.
- Related is the fact that Europeans, to pay for all these benefits, are willing to contribute 50, 60, or even 70 percent of their income in taxes to the state, whereas Americans have favored lower taxes, fewer public services, and more private disposable income.
- Europeans, operating from positions of military weakness, prefer negotiations and compromise on most foreign policy issues; the United States, the only global military superpower, has been much more inclined to use armed might.
- U.S. foreign policy, reflecting our domestic politics, is much more susceptible to interest group influence and political logrolling; in contrast, European foreign ministries, with their strong statist and bureaucratic traditions, are much more immunized from domestic pressures and interest groups.
- Europe, seemingly, favors peace at (almost) all costs; the United States is much more willing to take strong stands and use military might, if necessary.
- The Europeans, both out of relative weakness and genuine belief, prefer multilateral (EU, UN) solutions to international problems, while the Americans, as the only superpower, prefer to act alone.

It is important to emphasize that the United States and Europe are both products of a common Western cultural and social tradition: Greece, Rome, Christianity, the rule of law, limited government, capitalism, industrialization, the Enlightenment, rationalism, and democracy. We, therefore, share a certain common basis of understanding. Moreover, in the twentieth century's two great world wars, the Cold War, and through NATO and the Trans-Atlantic Alliance, we have been partners and allies for a long time, and those alliances will not be abandoned easily. Furthermore—and this is an important but often neglected factor in U.S.-European relations—the economic ties between the United States and Europe in the form of trade, investment, banking, joint ownership, business, and commerce are extensive. I have had European businessmen tell me that whatever political or foreign policy differences that may exist between the two regions are rendered largely irrelevant because our economic ties and financial interdependence are so great.

These economic, political, and cultural ties *are* still strong, probably stronger from the American perspective with Western Europe than with any other global area. Nevertheless, it is also clear that on the many religious, cultural, social, economic, and political dimensions listed earlier, the United States and Europe are drifting further and further apart. Inevitably, these social and political-cultural differences affect the two areas' foreign and strategic policies as well.

Here are some of the main foreign policy and strategic issues over which the United States and Western Europe disagree:

- Europe opposed Ronald Reagan's challenging, confrontational approach ("Mr. Gorbachev, 'Tear down this wall'") toward the Soviet Union; it much preferred negotiation over confrontation.
- For the same reason, it opposed the stationing of cruise missiles in Europe in the 1980s; it wanted a peaceful accommodation with the Soviets, not even the possibility of conflict or confrontation.
- In the 1990s, as the former Yugoslavia collapsed into violence and civil war, Europe, again favoring compromise and negotiation, could not get its act together sufficiently to take action; the United States in difficult areas such as Bosnia and Kosovo again had to come to Europe's rescue.
- Europe opposed strenuously George W. Bush's war in Iraq, seeing it as unnecessary and refusing to cooperate with us.
- Europe has sent troops to Afghanistan but mainly for noncombat missions; the United States has had to bear the main burden of war-fighting.
- Europe *overwhelmingly* favors negotiations to solve the conflicts over Iran's and North Korea's development of nuclear capacities; the United States has followed, again, a more confrontational approach.
- Shielded from domestic interest groups and public opinion, European foreign ministries are much more critical of Israel and favorable to the Palestinian cause than is the United States.

Thus, we see that, on almost every foreign policy and strategic issue, the United States and Western Europe, even operating from a common cultural history and linked background, are far apart. And increasingly more so.

Within this pattern, let us look at U.S. relations with individual European countries and regions and then with the EU itself.

France

France is a country of sixty-two million persons located in the heart of continental Europe, with a per capita income of $33,470 per year, making it one of the richest or most-developed countries in the world. It is an industrialized country, highly literate, highly urban, and very sophisticated in terms of its art, music, painting, and so on. Its capital, Paris, is one of the great cities in the world, a leader in business as well as livability.

For most of its history, France was one of the leading powers in the world, but its defeats in World Wars I and II led to its falling to the ranks of a secondary power. Nevertheless, the French language is still one of the world's leading international languages; French culture and art are world-renowned; France is a nuclear power; and the French arms industry and its military forces are among the world's top ten. France thinks of itself as a global power and its culture as universal.

Although France has by now fallen from the world power perch it occupied in past centuries, it is still a considerable power. The French, more than most, are sensitive to their fall from great-power ranks, and sometimes go to elaborate lengths to assert their importance and their independence. Under President Charles de Gaulle in the 1960s, France had withdrawn from NATO's military arm, only to return again in 2009 under President Nicolas Sarkozy; France had similarly often followed an independent (from the United States and from NATO) foreign policy.

France seeks to be an independent force in the world and often does not quite trust U.S. leadership and America's superpower status. It sees itself as both an ally and, at times, a check on U.S. power—as in Iraq, which France saw as a terrible mistake. At the same time, from the U.S. point of view, France has long been seen as a main check on the European continent against a resurgent Germany, as a loyal (in its own way) ally in the Cold War, and as a "civilizing" influence in helping to democratize first Southern Europe (Greece, Italy, Portugal, Spain) and now Eastern Europe.

Germany

Germany is the other great power alongside France in the heart of Europe. It is also a wealthy country with a per capita yearly income almost exactly that of France: $33,820. It is highly literate, an industrialized country, with highly advanced technology. Its gross national product is the fourth largest in the world, behind only the United States, China, and Japan. Like France, Germany is a beautiful country, lush and green, with advanced public services (health care, transportation), and yet a dynamic private sector. Although it once was on a par with France and Great Britain in terms of both population and productivity, now with the addition of the former communist East, Germany has considerably outstripped its historic rivals in size, population, and GNP.

And that is worrisome to its neighbors, if not to the United States. The problem is that Germany's history over the last century-and-a-half has often been one of aggression, war, and authoritarianism. Germany's neighbors, the victims of that aggression, have long tried to keep it calm and hem it in. That was one of the key reasons for the division of Germany after World War II, its incorporation into NATO, and the formation of the EU. As one commentator put it, the purpose of NATO in Europe was to keep the United States in, the Soviet Union out, and Germany divided. Hence, when Germany was united in 1991, it sent shockwaves through the capitals of Europe. A big, united, powerful Germany still raises alarms on the European continent.

Since World War II Germany has become peaceful, stable, and democratic. Everyone is pleased by Germany's democratic progress, its prosperity and stable middle class, and its incorporation into both NATO and the EU. The newer generations of Germans are much more liberal and far less authoritarian than were the older generations. But while the United States sees Germany as a loyal ally and a bulwark of stability and middle-of-the-road government, many Europeans still worry about Germany. Is it fully democratic and stable? Has German political culture really changed? Might a reunited and powerful Germany decide to go its own way, ignore NATO and the EU, and follow—once again—a more independent and aggressive foreign policy? The answer is: we think not, but we don't know for sure, and even asking the question, given Germany's earlier history, sets off alarm bells in Europe. Their attitude still is: beware an angry or unhappy Germany!

Great Britain

By almost all the indices we use—size, population, per capita income—the three main powers in Europe (France, Germany, Great Britain) were almost exactly equal. We use the past tense here because, since 1991 and the reunification, Germany has forged ahead in size, GNP, and power while France and Great Britain have lagged. The earlier power balance in Europe has been upset. That explains why, when East and West Germany were rejoined, both France and Great Britain opposed the move although they were unable to stop it. They feared a larger, more powerful, resurgent Germany might again become overly ambitious.

In the twentieth century, through two world wars, the Cold War, and now in the twenty-first century the war on terrorism, Great Britain has emerged as our closest ally. Much of American law, constitutionalism, and political practices are derived from Great Britain. So does our English language and much of our culture. Public opinion surveys reveal that Americans feel closer to Great Britain and have warmer feelings toward it than any other country except Canada. Those preferences have given rise to the only half-kidding aphorism that we like Great Britain, Canada, and Australia because we know that English-speaking countries are more trustworthy than any of the other kind.

Great Britain had been a declining society, country, and power at least since World War I. Its economy lagged behind other midlevel powers; its society was stiff and formal; and its strategic might left a lot to be desired. But Great Britain began to recover in the 1980s under Margaret Thatcher's leadership; oil finds in the nearby North Sea also helped Britain's recovery and turned it into a prosperous nation. Great Britain recovered its energy and spirit and proved during the 1990s and 2000s to be America's most loyal ally.

Great Britain was a junior partner in the relationship, however; it does not have the wealth, the population, or the military might any longer to be a global power. And many Brits look with skepticism on the country's close but secondary partnership with the United States, especially as British troops are killed alongside Americans in ill-conceived wars in Iraq and Afghanistan. They refer to Great Britain as America's "lap dog" or "poodle." Meanwhile, the British economy and political system are showing renewed signs of stagnation.

Southern Europe

Europe's peripheries can be divided in various ways. A common way to do so is in terms of Scandinavian or Nordic Europe, Southern or Mediterranean Europe, and Eastern Europe. In this chapter we briefly treat Southern and Nordic Europe; in the next chapter we deal with Eastern Europe, seeing it almost as a separate region.

Southern Europe in our definition includes four countries: Greece, Italy, Spain, and Portugal. France also has a long Mediterranean coast and is in some ways (religion, a part of its culture) a Southern European country. Albania and the countries of the former Yugoslavia (Slovenia, Croatia, Bosnia, Kosovo, Macedonia, Serbia) also border on or lie close to the Mediterranean, but they are very different culturally, politically, and economically and are studied in chapter three. Turkey may also be considered a Mediterranean country, but it is a Muslim-majority country and, therefore, different from these others. In the present analysis we treat only Greece, Italy, Spain, and Portugal.

Several features set these countries apart from Central or Northern Europe. First, they are historically Catholic or Greek Orthodox countries and their cultures and societies are very different from those of Northern Europe. Second, in terms of wealth and level of development, they lag behind the richer countries of Europe by about 10–20 percent in the cases of Greece, Italy, and Spain and by about 40 percent in the case of Portugal. Third, none of these countries could be considered a major power or even a middle-level one as are France, Germany, and Great Britain, but they are valuable in various ways as allies.

What makes these countries especially interesting for our purposes is the fact of their facing on, toward, and across the Mediterranean as well as toward Europe. Within Europe they are often treated as irrelevant inside NATO and the Trans-Atlantic Alliance; their economies are considered weaker than others in the Euro zone; and they are seldom counted on for military or strategic support in Eastern Europe or the Middle East. Of course, these condescending attitudes grate on the Southern Europeans who often resent their Northern European partners.

Across the Mediterranean they face North Africa (Morocco, Algeria, Tunisia, Egypt) as well as, not much farther away, sub-Saharan Africa. And that means Greece, Italy, Spain, and Portugal share a border (the Mediterranean) with and face the Third World in ways that Northern Europe does not. And they must, therefore, deal with a variety of issues stemming from their location—illegal immigration, the threat of terrorism, oil, poverty, drugs, racism, low literacy, disease, and so on—that are specific to the circum-Mediterranean.[3]

These issues affect their foreign policies as well. First, since the collapse of the Soviet Union and the end of the threat from the east, many NATO operations have moved to the Mediterranean and Southern Europe and the perceived threat from that area. Second, since the countries bordering on the Mediterranean Sea face many common problems—pollution of the waters, drug-running, trade in human beings—a number of new international organizations have sprung up in the area to deal with these common issues. And third, since this is one of the areas in the world where a rich area (Europe) faces and bumps up against a poor one (Africa), all kinds of conflicts, jealousies, envies, and misunderstandings are bound to develop. It is a situation not unlike that between the United States and Mexico—and giving rise to similar problems. I, therefore, recommend to the next generation of scholars greater focus on circum- and cross-Mediterranean studies since this is certain to be a global hotspot, give rise to all kinds of interesting issues, and to this point remains woefully understudied.

Northern Europe

Northern Europe, Scandinavia, or the Nordic countries, as they are variously known, consist of Norway, Sweden, Finland, and Denmark. Iceland may also be considered a part of this group, although it is very small and is geographically separated from the others by a thousand miles of ocean. Estonia would like to be considered a Scandinavian nation, and perhaps Latvia and Lithuania as well; but they are *much* poorer than the other Nordics, are different culturally and ethnically, and were long under Russian and Soviet control. It is possible that these three Baltic states will become rich and prosperous like their northern neighbors, but so far we prefer to treat them as part of Eastern Europe.

The four Nordics are among the richest and most prosperous on earth, with Norway leading the way and Denmark, Finland, and Sweden bunched together at about the same level as the rest of Western Europe. All four countries have been led in recent decades by mainly social-democratic parties and governments; all four have advanced social-welfare systems. All four have a wide range of public services and a very high standard of living. They are among the most comfortable, affluent, and happiest places in the world in which to live. To support all these services, the North Europeans also pay considerably more in income taxes than is the case in the United States. They are also much more communalist and collectivist than the more individualistic United States.

In foreign affairs the Nordics are much more committed to multilateralism, to achieving peace through negotiations and diplomacy, than is the more confrontational United States. We often think of them as peace-mongers, antimilitary, antinuclear weapons, and frequently anti-American. For that reason the Scandinavians have been wary of joining NATO (only Denmark is a member) and especially its military arm, although they are not opposed to political cooperation through the Trans-Atlantic Alliance. Lying closer to Russia and even bordering on it (Norway and Finland), the Nordics are also more fearful than the United States of antagonizing the powerful Russian bear.

But this reputation for nonconfrontation and peace-mongering has not prevented the Nordics from following some pretty tough policies where needed. First, their internal police and security forces are very disciplined, well-trained, and tough: do not get caught in Scandinavia trying to sell drugs or bringing in illegal immigrants. Second, the Northern countries have been very good in providing training in border patrol, immigration control, and police to their neighbors across the Baltic—Estonia, Latvia, and Lithuania. That helps both "the Balts" and the Nordics keep the Russians at bay; it also relieves the United States and NATO from having to do that sensitive work.

The EU

The EU grew out of the European Community (EC), which, in turn, grew out of the European Steel and Coal Community. As the names suggest, the EU began as a trade agreement, grew into an economic common market, and is now not just an economic but also a cultural, social, political, diplomatic, and security/military union.

The trouble was for a long time the EU had no diplomatic corps or military force under its command. It lacked political or strategic weight. To implement its resolutions it required the military or strategic contributions of its member states. This dilemma was best captured by U.S. secretary of state Henry Kissinger's famous question: "When I want to call 'Europe,' what number should I use?" By which Kissinger meant that he knew whom to call in the foreign or defense ministries in London, Paris, or Bonn; but if he was trying to reach a foreign minister or defense minister for "Europe," there was no such number.

This problem plagued Europe for years and even decades. The problem was that the bigger European countries were willing to give up some of their sovereignty over economic and trade matters but, when it came to foreign or defense matter, they preferred to carry out their own individual national policies and not subsume those to some vague "European" policy.

It took the wars in the former Yugoslavia in the early 1990s for this to change. There, while Europe dithered and each individual country (Austria, France, Germany, Italy) sought to advance its own national self-interest in the region, some of the worst slaughters, genocides, and tortures in Europe since World War II were taking place. Europe dithered so long, unable to reach agreement, and so disgracefully that eventually the United States had to intervene militarily to stop the slaughter, bail out the Europeans, and restore a degree of order (the "Dayton Accords") to the region.

It is out of this disgraceful series of events that the Europeans decided to create a Europe-wide office responsible for foreign policy and another, separate from NATO, for defense policy. That action also solved the quip originally raised by Kissinger: now there was a telephone number to call (actually two of them) if we needed to consult "Europe" on foreign or defense matters.

But these steps did not resolve the key underlying issues. First, even though we now have a "foreign minister" for Europe, that person still has only a small staff at her disposal, has no embassies abroad, and cannot take any action without clearing it first with the major member states. The same, and even more so, with defense policy: although there now is a "defense minister" for Europe, he has no or very few troops at his disposal, no guns to deploy, and must consult with the individual members before taking any action. Even more than with foreign policy, defense policy is still strictly under the control of the member national governments. In addition, the European defense minister lives in an uneasy relationship both with NATO and with the U.S. European Command (CENTCOM).

The foregoing analysis illustrates the problem of a group of states, even those as closely linked as those in Europe, coming together to present a common foreign or defense policy. While on some issues they can act together, on the more difficult ones they still operate largely as unilateral actors. That is truer of bigger states (France, Germany, Great Britain) than it is of smaller ones. Interviews conducted by the author revealed, for example, that while up to 80 percent of Danish foreign policy is also EU foreign policy, only 40 percent of German policy is in full correspondence with EU policy.

As a result of this complicated situation, the United States has to maintain a dual-track policy in dealing with Europe: one aimed at the EU as a collective entity and the other, in the traditional manner, directed toward individual countries. Meanwhile, as we see in more detail in the next chapter, the doubling of Europe's size to now include twenty-seven members, in both Western and Eastern Europe, has changed the very definition of what we mean by "Europe." Europe is presently divided right down the middle, with the Eastern countries often more supportive of U.S. policies than our historic and erstwhile allies in the West. These changes have placed new pressures on the already fragile U.S.-European relationship.

Conclusion

The United States and Western Europe are drifting apart, not because of some large shock but gradually over time. Though most of our culture, language, family origins, and political institutions derive from Europe, those ties are being forgotten and are generally weakening. They are weakening for a variety of reasons: European values and priorities are increasingly different from our own; America itself is becoming more multicultural and is no longer so closely tied to Europe; and we have lost our main reason for working together—containing the Soviet Union. Obviously we will continue to work closely in the future with our European allies on a variety of issues, and our economic and cultural ties remain strong. Nevertheless, other areas (Asia, the Middle East, Latin America) have gained in priority often at Europe's expense, there are tensions in our relations with Europe, and socially and culturally Europe and the United States have increasingly gone their separate ways.

These broad social and cultural changes within Europe inevitably have a major impact on foreign policy. Since Europe is now so rich, as well off as the United States, Europe tends to feel it does not need the United States for much anymore. It no longer *depends* on the United States as it did in earlier periods. At the same time, Western Europe increasingly views the United States condescendingly as a "cowboy" nation, reckless and impetuous (as in Iraq), not to be fully trusted with all the military power that we have. Many Europeans now think it is the United States and its power that need to be contained, not Russia, Iran, or Al Qaeda as we think. European opinions of the United States have steadily declined in recent decades; at the same time, European reliance on American might and leadership has diminished.

The growing gaps and tensions between Europe and the United States are bound to have an impact on the transatlantic alliance and its institutions. Is it even appropriate to speak of a "transatlantic alliance" anymore if the alliance is so frayed? What usefulness (limited) does an institution like NATO have if its primary purpose—containing the Soviet Union—has disappeared? Why do we still keep large numbers of troops and military bases in Western Europe, at huge expense, if there is nothing there (the old, now disbanded, Warsaw Pact) for them to defend against?

We know from our domestic politics that old bureaucracies (like the Department of Commerce) seldom die or disappear even after their usefulness has run out; the same applies to foreign affairs. As the United States and Western Europe continue to drift apart, however, it makes little sense for us to maintain all of those agencies that were useful in one era, the Cold War, but are no longer so in the present. The issue of U.S. troops in Europe, the many U.S. bases there, NATO, the Atlantic Council, and a host of U.S. schools, training programs, and joint exercises in Europe have all become anachronistic or nearly so. We need to put our relations with Europe on a new, more pragmatic, and more realistic basis to reflect new times and new issues, not the old Cold War, which is definitively over. The only question is whether we make these changes now and on a rational basis or we allow these anachronistic institutions to linger on indefinitely not only past their time of usefulness but when the United States as a nation can no longer afford them.

Notes

1. Samuel P. Huntington, *Who Are We? The Challenge to America's National Identity* (New York: Simon and Schuster, 2004).
2. Robert Kagan, *Of Paradise and Power: America and Europe in the New World Order* (New York: Knopf, 2003).
      But see also Dennis Bark. *Americans and Europeans Dancing in the Dark* (Stanford, CA: Hoover Institution Press, 2007).
3. An interesting parallel is the U.S. border with Mexico where, similarly, a rich, First World country faces across the Rio Grande a poor, Third World country, and all the problems to which such stark contrasts give rise.

Suggested Readings

Bark, Dennis. *Americans and Europeans Dancing in the Dark* (Stanford, CA: Hoover Institution Press, 2007).

Davies, Norman. *A History of Europe* (Oxford, UK: Oxford University Press, 1996).

Hancock, Donald et al. *Politics in Europe* (New York: Chatham House Press, 2003).

Kagan, Robert. *Of Paradise and Power: America and Europe in the New World Order* (New York: Knopf, 2003).

Kesselman, Mark et al. *European Politics in Transition* (Boston: Houghton Mifflin, 1997).

Kircher, Emil J. (ed.). *Liberal Parties in Western Europe* (Cambridge, UK: Cambridge University Press, 1988).

Lewis, Flora. *Europe: A Tapestry of Nations* (New York: Simon and Schuster, 1987).

Tiersky, Ronald (ed.). *Europe Today* (Lanham, MS: Rowman and Littlefield, 1999).

Treverton, Gregory (ed.). *The Shape of the New Europe* (New York: Council on Foreign Relations, 1992).

Wiarda, Howard J. (ed.). *European Politics in the Age of Globalization* (Fort Worth: Harcourt Publishers, 2001).

Zelikow, Philip and Condoleeza Rice. *Germany Unified and Europe Transformed* (Cambridge, UK: Cambridge University Press, 1995).

CHAPTER 3

Eastern Europe

Eastern Europe is one of the subregions of Europe, rather like Southern Europe (Greece, Italy, Portugal, Spain) or Northern or Scandinavian Europe (Denmark, Finland, Norway, Sweden). Most of Eastern Europe has now joined the two great European "clubs," the European Union (EU) and the North Atlantic Treaty Organization (NATO); but because the Eastern countries have a distinct history and were for so long under the control of the Soviet Union, they deserve separate treatment in this chapter.

Several features make Eastern Europe distinguishable from the rest of Europe. First, Eastern Europe, like Southern or Northern Europe, was for a long time on the periphery of the great currents of Western history: the Renaissance, the Enlightenment, the Industrial Revolution, and the movement toward democratic government. It missed out on many of the great movements that led to the modern age. And second and related, Eastern Europe is considerably poorer than the rest of Europe. It lacks the affluence, the style, the rich social programs that we associate with Western Europe. In fact, there is a rule that applies generally in this part of the world that says: the farther east in Europe you go, the poorer it becomes. Though we often expect to see poverty, malnutrition, and disease in Africa, Latin America, and South and Southeast Asia, when we see such poverty in Europe it is doubly shocking because we don't expect to see it there.

A third reason for Eastern Europe's distinctiveness is its forty-five-year subordination, until 1991, to the Soviet Union and its organization into the Warsaw Pact and Comecon, Moscow's response to NATO and the EU. More recently, Eastern Europe has been freed from Russia's yoke and is seeking to join the world of modern, developed European states; but it has not yet fully consolidated its new democratic status and it is still subject to Russian pressures. Because of these vulnerabilities, the Eastern European states are often closer in their foreign policies to the United States, whom they see as their protector, than they are to their nearer Western European neighbors.

For a long time, students of comparative and international politics divided the world into three great blocs: the First World of modern, developed states; the Second World of developed communist (which included Eastern Europe) states; and a Third World of new or emerging nations.[1] But now we know that classification, because of Soviet secretiveness and lies, was wrong. Both Russia and Eastern Europe, it has been revealed since the tearing up of the Iron Curtain dividing East from West, were, and are, far poorer than we had thought. They were *not* "developed" communist states but underdeveloped ones, often closer to the Third World than to the First. The poverty of the East and Russia came as a shock to those in the West who for many decades were unable to travel freely in the East and who were not cognizant of how badly off the East was.

While the earlier "Second World" designation was wrong and misleading, I have chosen to continue using that term here, but to redefine it. What we mean in this book by "Second World" is not "developed" communist states but states that are in transition from communism to democracy and development, and have not yet completed that transition. They are no longer "Third World" but they have not yet made it to "First World" status either. Rather, they are stuck in between. Moreover, they show certain distinctive features of this transitional status: weak and unconsolidated democracies, fragile economies, underdeveloped infrastructure (roads, highways, electricity, bridges, transportation, port facilities), and bureaucracies and governments (including, importantly, the armed forces) that do not work very well. Eastern Europe has a very long way to go to make it up to West European levels.

Even though their transitions are still incomplete, most of the Eastern European countries—Estonia, Latvia, Lithuania, Poland, the Czech Republic, Hungary, Slovenia, Slovakia, Bulgaria, and

Romania—have now become members of the EU and NATO. They are part of "Europe," writ large, even while not yet fully integrated into it. But now the question arises, "Where Does Europe End?" Where is the eastern and southeastern border of Europe?

A few years ago, when I was living in Eastern Europe and studying European enlargement, it was generally conceded that Europe ended at roughly the same line that it did in 1919—that is, at the end of World War I and before the Soviet Union's World War II era expansion into and subjugation of this area. It thus included the three Baltic states of Estonia, Latvia, and Lithuania, Poland, Czechoslovakia (before their division into the two states of the Czech Republic and Slovakia), Hungary, Romania, and Bulgaria. Albania and Yugoslavia and its present-day component parts were, then as now, up for grabs.

But now such countries even farther to the east (and thus often even poorer) as Belarus, the Ukraine, Moldova, and Georgia are also clamoring to join NATO and the EU. And so is Turkey, a large and predominantly Muslim country that borders on the Middle East. The United States wants these countries into NATO and the EU because it assists us in the war on terrorism and puts a tighter perimeter around Russia and slams the door on future Russian expansionism, but our European allies are not much in favor of further enlargement because to bring these countries up to acceptable standards will mean huge subsidies for which the Europeans will have to pay.

At the same time, Russia does not want NATO, which was born as an anti-Russian alliance after all, so close that, as the Russians put it, it is at the gates of Moscow. So now we are faced with a series of new dilemmas: how far east and south should NATO and the EU go; how much of these countries' burden of underdevelopment is the West willing to take on; and how far east can the Western alliance extend before it bumps up against a resentful (for having lost the Cold War) and resurgent (with abundant oil and natural gas wealth) Russia determined, perhaps forcefully, to resist any further Western expansion into what it considers Russia's sphere of influence. Or, before it runs up against the Middle East and its problems.

There are many interesting and important issues here. We begin in this chapter with a consideration of Eastern Europe and how its incorporation into the West involves both opportunities and challenges. In the next chapter we deal with Russia itself and how the eastern progression of NATO and the EU presents immense challenges to that country too.

Background

Eastern Europe, on the periphery of the Continental European Core Area (France, Germany, Belgium, the Netherlands, Switzerland, Austria), has long been poorer than the rest of Europe. It lagged behind in terms of industrialization, social change, and democratization.

In addition, Eastern Europe has long been severely buffeted about by its larger and more powerful neighbors. This has also prevented both economic growth and the institutionalization that would lead to strong nationhood. This "buffeting about" has been both cultural-religious and political-strategic. On the cultural-religious front, Eastern Europe has long been torn between the democracies and representative governments of the West, and the absolutist-authoritarian regimes of the East (czarist Russia) and South (the Ottoman Empire). Militarily and strategically, Eastern Europe lay between the great expansionist powers of Austria, Germany, Russia, and the Ottomans and in the path of their conquests.

Table 3.1 provides data for a comparative understanding of the East European countries and their level of development. The World Bank uses two different indices of per capita income: gross national income (GNI—income from both domestic production and foreign sources) and PPP GNI, which is purchasing power parity or GNI adjusted for international differences in prices. I have to say, I don't trust the PPP index. It tends to boost the numbers up above what they really are. From my travels and research in the area, I believe Eastern Europe is considerably poorer than these numbers show. I think these numbers have been "cooked" to show Eastern Europe in a more favorable light than is actually the case and to disguise from the West Europeans how much they will have to pay in taxes and the subsidies to bring the East up to European standards.

But for now, let us take these figures as they are—at face value. Note that the average for the Eastern European countries that have recently been admitted to the EU and NATO is slightly under $10,000 per person per year. Seven of the twenty-five countries listed are rated as high income (but usually just barely above that threshold);

Table 3.1 Gross national income (GNI) per capita

Country	GNI (in $)	Category
Albania	3,620	LMC
Armenia	2,640	LMC
Azerbaijan	2,550	LMC
Belarus	4,220	UMC
Bosnia	6,150	LMC
Bulgaria	4,590	UMC
Croatia	10,460	UMC
Cyprus	24,940	HIC
Czech Republic	14,450	HIC
Estonia	13,200	HIC
Georgia	2,120	LMC
Hungary	11,570	HIC
Latvia	9,930	UMC
Lithuania	9,920	UMC
Macedonia	3,460	LMC
Malta	15,310	HIC
Moldova	1,260	LMC
Poland	9,840	UMC
Romania	6,150	UMC
Russia	7,560	UMC
Serbia	4,730	UMC
Slovakia	11,730	HIC
Slovenia	20,960	HIC
Turkey	8,020	UMC
Ukraine	2,550	LMC

HIC = High-income country (above $11,456); UMC = Upper-middle-income country ($3,706–11,456); LMC = Lower-middle-income country ($936–3,705).

ten are upper middle income; eight are lower middle income. Malta, Cyprus, Slovenia, the Czech Republic, and Estonia are at the high end of that scale; Bulgaria and Romania are at the low end; and Latvia, Lithuania, and Poland are about in the middle. Remember that these are *averages*; they do not show the extreme poverty that still exists in some areas of these countries.

But note also the average of under $10,000 makes these countries only about one-third to one-fourth as wealthy as most of the countries of Western Europe or the United States, with a long way to go to (if ever) catch up. If we take the comparison further afield, we note that most of the countries of Eastern Europe are no better off than the relatively successful countries of Latin America (Brazil, Chile, Mexico), which are still considered developing or Third World countries.

If we look at the present candidates for admission to the European club, they are poorer still. Only Croatia has the present wealth to compare with the rest of Eastern Europe (its candidacy has been held up by its unwillingness to hand over war criminals to the international criminal court in The Hague). Meanwhile, the other current candidates—Albania, Macedonia, Bosnia, Kosovo (for which we have no figures as yet), and Serbia—are way down the list in terms of wealth and are definitely at Third World levels. It will take an enormous effort (and money) to bring them up to European standards.

Then, if we look at the countries—Belarus, Georgia, Moldova, Armenia, Azerbaijan, the Ukraine—that are future candidates (at least in their own eyes) for EU and NATO admission, the situation is even more dire. These are very poor countries. Not only are they poor, but, in keeping with our "Second World" description, they are also disorganized, chaotic, and lacking infrastructure. They are not at the upper reaches of the Third World as was the last group of countries to be admitted, but at the lower levels. They are among the poorer of the poor, at the level of Bolivia, Honduras, or Paraguay. Can one imagine these countries being admitted to Europe?

For this to happen, which the United States favors on strategic grounds (military bases, oil, better access to Iraq and Afghanistan), it would require decades and *generations* of effort on the Europeans' part and truly massive doses of foreign aid and subsidies. Such subsidies in the present circumstances of economic crisis in the developed countries are unlikely to be forthcoming. So maybe we *do*, in fact, know where Europe ends: it ends with the Baltic states, Poland, Slovakia, Romania, Bulgaria, and the Balkans, but it does not include anything to the east of that, including Belarus, Georgia, Armenia, Azerbaijan, Moldova, the Ukraine, and certainly not Russia except perhaps in some future "associated" (not full) membership.

The problem in Eastern Europe, therefore, wherever we finally draw that line demarking EU and NATO member states, is both a strategic one and a developmental one. The strategic issue is that the farther east NATO and the EU go, the closer they come to the gates of Moscow, thus antagonizing Russia and threatening Russia's own security interests. The developmental issue stems from the fact that these are still poor, underdeveloped, not well-institutionalized countries. And the two factors are closely interrelated: to the extent that Eastern Europe remains poor and weak, it also remains vulnerable to Russian pressures, exercised through the absolute dependence of most of these countries on Russian oil and natural gas to heat their homes and run their factories, and even through the ever-present possibility that the far larger Russian armies will simply march across their territories and take them over as they did at the initiation of the Cold War in the 1940s.

U.S. Interests and Policies

Eastern Europe lacks the grand, triumphal history of the Western European countries. Eastern Europe was never a part of the ancient Greek empire and its advanced art and learning, never a part of the Roman Empire and its civilizing (language, law, government, religion, social organization) mission. Nor does Eastern Europe have the large, grandiloquent, nation-building history to be proud of in France, Germany, Great Britain, Italy, Spain, and even Denmark and Sweden who were once great powers with large empires. Instead, Eastern Europe remained on the sidelines or periphery of Europe, came late to Christianity and civilization, and was always less-developed sociologically and politically as well as economically as compared with its rich neighbors to the West. An unsettled area with constantly fluctuating borders, it was frequently overrun and devastated by outside, marauding armies: Russians, Magyars, Turks, Napoleon, Germans, Mongolians, Swedes, Danes, and Austrians.

This is not to say that Eastern European history is uninteresting; on the contrary, it is very interesting and we commend it to a whole generation of rising, young historians. What it lacks is not interesting themes and issues but in modern times the sense of triumph, victory, and great deeds accomplished that is characteristic of the large and largely successful states of Western Europe. Instead, Eastern European history is characterized by despair, defeat, frustration, and marginalization as an area peripheral to the great social, economic, and political currents that emerged in the West. The only thing comparable in the East is the great Polish-Lithuanian Empire of the fifteenth century, which stretched all the way from the Baltic to the Black Sea, but it did not last and its accomplishments were not permanent.

As Western Europe began to enter the modern world (science, technology, the Renaissance, capitalism, Protestantism, social change, representative government) in the sixteenth century, Eastern Europe lagged behind. It was bypassed by all these currents and others that we associate with the making of the modern world: the Enlightenment, the industrial revolution, the gradual movement toward limited and democratic government. Most of Eastern Europe failed to modernize; it remained locked in the embrace of feudalism and the Middle Ages, and it was even more marginalized than before. It lagged further and further behind the rest of Europe and, rather like Southern Europe, developed some large inferiority complexes.

On the international front, no great or even major power developed in the modern era in Eastern Europe. Poland "disappeared" during the entire nineteenth century, carved up and absorbed by the other great powers: Germany, Russia, and Austria. The Austro-Hungarian Empire, long weaker than its large territory suggested, was defeated in World War I and broken up into the smaller nation-states of Austria, Czechoslovakia, and Hungary.

The Ottoman Empire similarly disappeared in World War I, pulling back to its base in Asia Minor (Turkey) but leaving behind pockets of Muslim communities (Albania, Bosnia, Kosovo) that would retard South-East Europe's development. Even Russia, engulfed in revolution after 1917, retreated from its earlier enlarged boundaries, allowing the Baltic states of Estonia, Latvia, and Lithuania, plus a resurgent Poland and the rest of Eastern Europe to enjoy a twenty–year (1919–1939), long-delayed period of peace and independence.

World War II (1939–1945) and its aftermath in the late 1940s was a disastrous time for Eastern Europe and for U.S. and West European interests in the region. In the course of halting, reversing, and then rolling back the German/Fascist invasion of Russia, the large Russian armies marched into and occupied all three of the Baltic countries. They also occupied Poland, Hungary, Czechoslovakia, Bulgaria, Romania, and about 40 percent of Germany.

The Balkans were forcefully pacified under a similarly brutal communist government headed by Josip Tito allied to the Soviet Union and now called, somewhat artificially, Yugoslavia. Both Austria and Finland, Russia's other proximate neighbors in the West, avoided full-scale Soviet occupation by proclaiming their neutrality in the Cold War and allowing the Soviet Union certain privileged rights within their territories. At the end of World War II and in the immediate ensuing years, Eastern Europe, either as a collective or as a group of independent states, had disappeared once again, enveloped within the totalitarian embrace of the Soviet Union.

Thus began the Cold War between the West and the Soviet Union in the place where it was largely concentrated for the next forty-five years: Eastern Europe. U.S. policy in the region during this nearly half a century was a complete disaster. At high-level conferences in Potsdam, Tehran, and Yalta, for the sake of ending World War II quickly and securing an accommodation with the Soviets, the United States and the West European allies essentially acquiesced in the Soviet Union's occupation of Eastern Europe. We called them "captured nations" and *talked* about rolling back the Iron Curtain and tearing down the Berlin Wall dividing East from West, but when push came to shove we did nothing about it. In the several showdowns—in 1956 in Hungary, in 1961 in Berlin, and in 1969 in Prague—when Soviet brutality was under attack and appeared to be toppling, the United States stood by and did nothing, allowing brave freedom fighters to be mowed down by Soviet guns. Eastern Europe was betrayed; it was a disgrace.

Meantime, the entire apparatus of the Cold War was constructed and revved up. When we created NATO in the West, the Soviets created the Warsaw Pact in Eastern Europe; both alliances were armed to the teeth. When Western Europe created the European Community, later the European Union, Russia created the Comecon. When we helped rearm the French, West Germans, British, and others, the Russians armed the Poles, Czechs, Hungarians, Bulgarians, Romanians, and East Germans. When we created spy agencies such as the CIA, NSA, and others, the Soviets created intelligence agencies in all their East European satellites. Fearful that the Soviet Union might advance even farther into Europe, we established the doctrine of "Containment" to prevent that from happening.

The result for almost all of those years was a standoff: the border between East and West bristled with armies and armaments; nuclear weapons on both sides prevented either alliance from advancing (the "nuclear terror"), and the United States and its NATO allies and the Soviets and their Warsaw Pact allies stood toe-to-toe along this long border for over four decades. Meanwhile (although that is not the focus of this chapter), the main Cold War battlefields began to shift away from Europe and toward the Third World—China, Korea, Cuba, the Congo, Vietnam and Southeast Asia, Central America, the Horn of Africa. Tensions along the Iron Curtain eased or at least reached a stalemate.

While there was stalemate at the strategic and military level, at the underlying social, cultural, economic, and political level there was considerable dynamism; things began to change. First, during the 1980s it became apparent that the Soviet economy could not compete with those of the United States and its allies; over time the Soviets began to pull back from providing massive financial and other assistance to their East European allies. Second, although the Soviets tried to disguise the fact, eventually it became obvious that living standards in the West were so much higher—often five–six times as high—than those in the East that they could no longer be denied. And that triggered a massive sentiment in the East that they, too, ought to be able to enjoy the affluence and good life that those in the West had. Third, especially among East European youth, inspired by rock music, the youth protests of the 1960s and 1970s, and the worldwide desire among youth for greater freedom and fewer restrictions, an entire generation of East European young people began to clamor for an end to censorship, freedom to travel, and better job and living opportunities. When these forces came together in the mid-to-late-1980s, the once-mighty Soviet empire and its satellites in Eastern Europe began to tremble.

In addition to the economic crisis of which we've already spoken, the moral and intellectual crisis of communism, and the youth or generational crisis, there also began to be a political challenge to long-standing communist/Soviet rule. Leading the way were Poland's Solidarity Movement and Czechoslovakia's Charter 29. These movements built on the rising discontent and, often assisted with U.S. democracy-promotion funds, began to challenge communist authorities. These "civil society" organizations, in turn, gave rise to other protests and protest movements in the several Eastern European countries. It is not our purpose here to recount all of that history, only to emphasize the general patterns. And that involved a slowly building crescendo of opposition to Soviet rule, a de-legitimization of the communist ideology, an unwillingness to work anymore for, let alone support, their communist masters, coupled with rising protest movements, strikes, marches, and work stoppages. Eventually, this hollowed-out system could not function any more and, having lost all legitimacy as well as the ability to pay for its vast empire, the puppet regimes established by the Soviet Union began to crumble and the Soviet forces prepared to withdraw. Between 1989 and 1991 (the final collapse of the old Soviet system), Eastern Europe freed itself from forty-five years of Soviet rule.

Immediately, the question became: what should now happen in Eastern Europe? At the time there were a number of proposals: make Eastern Europe into a neutral zone between Russia and the West, establish some sort of guardianship by the closest and most affected Western nations (France, Germany, Sweden, Austria, Italy) over the East, or allow the Eastern nations to go in the direction that they themselves preferred, which was toward the West, NATO, and the EU. Neither of the first two solutions made any sense and/or was unmanageable from an international perspective; de facto, the third solution became the only practical one.

Both NATO (largely run by the United States) and the EU (largely run by the European countries but with strong U.S. influence) began to draw up plans to have the newly liberated East European countries admitted to their clubs. The requirements included the establishment of democracy in Eastern Europe, a better human rights record after the strict controls of the Soviet era, reform and privatization (capitalism) of these formerly socialist economies, infrastructure reform (education, governance, public administration), and, in the case of NATO, military reform. It should be emphasized that all these are *major* changes, not just mere tinkering, involving wholesale changes in how these countries were run and fundamental or systemic renovation. The EU set forth eighty thousand changes in the *acquis comunitaire* that needed to be made; through the Partnership for Peace (PfP), NATO's requirements were almost as stringent.

The trouble is, recall, these are very poor countries. They are also underdeveloped. They did not and do not have the funds available for such a wholesale restructuring. Nor did any of them have any experience in democratic self-government or a modern, free-market economy. They did not have political parties, independent labor unions, business associations, or civil society; all this would have to be created from scratch. They lacked the infrastructure for development and their governments and bureaucracies, still often operating in the old Soviet style, were inefficient, bloated, corrupt, and not oriented toward serving the public. Their political culture was still cast in the top-down, authoritarian, Soviet mold; they had no experience in the give-and-take of modern, democratic, participatory politics. This would all have to mean nation-building at its most fundamental level, from the ground up.

What to do? Something would eventually have to give since the countries involved were so inadequately prepared. Both the United States and the Europeans poured in enormous amounts of foreign aid. The Americans and the Europeans also invested heavily in the East with, among the Europeans, an interesting division of labor that reflected the historic interests of the Western countries in the Eastern ones: Denmark and Sweden in the Baltics, Germany in Poland and the Czech Republic, Austria in Hungary (part of Austria's former empire), France in Romania, and Italy in Slovenia. In the United States, campaigns were undertaken to mobilize the ethnic communities of these various countries (Poles, Slovaks, etc.) both to invest and put resources into their former home countries and to lobby to have Congress approve their admission to NATO.[2]

The result was something of a farce on all sides. Both the EU and NATO had strict criteria for admission. But it soon became apparent that, under these criteria, *none* of the East European countries could quality. None were really prepared for membership. But if they weren't admitted, the chances were good that the East Europeans would fall (i) into chaos or (ii) back into the arms of Russia. Since that couldn't be allowed, the East European countries were admitted to the EU and NATO even though they were not fully qualified. With regard to the EU, the rule became: if they just enact the *legislation* that showed that *legally* they were in accord with the eighty thousand requirements, that was good enough; they were not required to actually implement the legislation. Similarly with regard to NATO: Eastern Europe had to *formally* comply by reforming their defense ministries and systems *on paper*; implementation was left to a later date.

The logic behind these arguments was that it was better to have these countries, even though unqualified, "inside the tent" (of NATO and the EU) rather than outside where the United States and Western Europe would have no leverage. But the real reasons were strategic: (i) fear that Eastern Europe would fall into economic and political chaos, and (ii) that Russia would take advantage of their weakness to once again suck them up into its orbit. In actual fact, however, by admitting unqualified new members to NATO and the EU, the United States and West Europe lost most of their leverage over them since, with their key goals—membership in the EU and NATO—achieved, they no longer had any incentives to continue to reform. Be that as it may, in one "big bang," NATO and the EU increased their membership by ten (going from north to south): Estonia, Latvia, Lithuania, Poland, the Czech Republic, Slovakia, Hungary, Malta, Cyprus, Slovenia, and then added Bulgaria and Romania shortly thereafter.

The admission of all these new countries to the EU and NATO changed the dynamics of these two institutions in important ways:

1. Most obviously, both organizations became larger and more unwieldy in terms of making decisions.
2. Europe's security perimeter was now suddenly extended several hundred miles to the east and that much closer to Russia.
3. The EU and NATO consisted not just of wealthy, developed nations but now of poor, developing ones as well.
4. The poverty of the East would require *massive* U.S. and European subsidies, now and indefinitely into the future, to bring them up to even minimal levels.
5. The East European countries, mindful of the continuing Russian threat and seeing the United States as their only military protector, were more inclined to side with the United States in international disputes than with Western ("Old") Europe. These divisions often split Europe (e.g., on Iraq or Afghanistan) and split the Trans-Atlantic Alliance.
6. The United States, understanding this split, was often able to play off Eastern Europe versus Western Europe and thus get what it wanted out of both NATO and the EU.

While these tensions remained, Eastern Europe was now "safely" inside the EU and NATO. Seeing their success and the rewards (a higher standard of living, jobs and investment, military modernization) that flow from it, other nations even farther east have begun to clamor for admission. But these nations (Moldova, Belarus, Georgia, Armenia, Azerbaijan, and the Ukraine) are even less qualified than the previous group was. And not only are they closer to Russia, they are also, unlike the previous entrants, countries that were long a part of Russia and that Russia still considers part of "Greater Russia." So the admission of these countries to NATO and the EU is bound to antagonize Russia even more than the previous round did and to lead to some serious, if not military, confrontations.

From the point of view of U.S. security and interests, it makes sense for us to expand the EU and NATO into Eastern Europe for the following reasons:

- We want a stable and prosperous Eastern Europe.
- We want a democratic and human rights–observing Eastern Europe.
- We want an Eastern European security perimeter around a reconstituted, nationalistic, surly, and aggressive Russia.

But even a good policy has its limits. Should we also incorporate Belarus, Georgia, Moldova, Armenia, Azerbaijan, and the Ukraine? Should that security perimeter spoken of earlier extend almost literally to the gates of Moscow and the Kremlin? Or should we also include Russia, bring it, too, " inside the tent"? Probably not. But where do we draw the line? And what if the citizens of these countries, aspiring to be democratic, vote that they would rather be part of the West than the East? These are truly tough political and strategic questions.

In the next section we look at the several subregions of Eastern Europe, enabling us to analyze various countries and groups of countries specifically and in more detail.

Regional Variations

The Baltic

The three Baltic states of Estonia, Latvia, and Lithuania are the north-ernmost of the East European countries. All three are small (three to five million persons), lacking in significant natural resources, and extremely vulnerable to Russian pressures. There are significant differences as well as similarities between the three countries; you could have your own interesting area studies program here.

Estonia is the most northern of the three. It is ethnically and linguistically closest to Finland, mainly Protestant (Lutheran), and likes to think of itself as a Scandinavian country, even though it has a large (30–35 percent) and still unassimilated Russian minority. Lithuania is the southernmost of the three, mainly Catholic, only 7 percent Russian, and oriented toward Poland and Germany. Latvia is in between, a mix ethnically and religiously, and its Russian population (35–40 percent) is better educated and more assimilated.

All three countries are extremely susceptible to Russian manipulation. They are all dependent on Russia for oil and natural gas; Russian armies (which outnumber their own by about forty to one) are parked right on their borders; and Russia still often considers this area part of "Greater Russia." The Russian minorities inside these countries constitute a "Fifth Column" who often refuse to learn the national language of their host country and whose loyalties would be suspect in case of a crisis. The economic crisis currently affecting all the Baltic countries makes them especially vulnerable.

The United States and Western Europe have aided these three countries with foreign assistance and investment and by bringing them into the EU and NATO. Especially interesting for our purposes is that the other Scandinavian countries have aided "the Balts" with border control, police training, and immigration control obviously aimed at keeping Russia at bay and relieving the United States and NATO from having to fulfill those functions.

You have to admire the Balts—three plucky little nations standing up against the pressures of the big Russian bear. Obviously we want them to remain democratic, to succeed in their goal to achieve economic development, and to be successfully integrated into EU and NATO. But what if Russia steps up the pressure or, at some point, decides to reconquer this territory that once belonged to it? Then, other than through diplomacy, how much would the United States, the Europeans, or all of us together in NATO be willing to commit militarily to defend these all-but-defenseless countries?

Central Europe

For our purposes, Central Europe, or perhaps better, East-Central Europe, consists of Poland, the Czech Republic, Hungary, and Slovakia. When the Soviet Empire broke up in 1991, the Czech Republic and Slovakia were still united in a single nation called Czechoslovakia, but the Slovaks were tired of being second-class citizens in this arrangement, and, in the so-called Velvet (smooth) Revolution, became an independent country. Austria likes to think of itself as the capital of Central Europe since most of the territory encompassed in these other four nations was once part of the Austro-Hungarian Empire; but Austria is a wealthy nation (not "Second World"), was not a Soviet satellite,[3] and considers itself a *West* European nation, not *East* European. It should not be considered in the same category as the other four.

Although their democracies and economies are still vulnerable, especially in the current economic downturn, Poland, the Czech Republic, Hungary, and Slovakia should be considered among the bright spots in Eastern Europe. All four are significant and viable nations; all have major agriculture as well as industry and other resources; and all have established democracy and begun a process of economic reform. But they have major problems yet of government inefficiency, bureaucratic corruption, and underdeveloped infrastructure. We can see from table 3.1 that the Czech Republic is the best off of the four due to its educated population and its proximity to Germany; Slovakia is the least developed; while Poland and Hungary are in between.

Although all four countries were occupied by the Soviet Union from World War II on, they all had independent histories of their own and were never considered part of Great Russia. In fact, the Soviet Union saw them as buffer states to guard it against future German or NATO expansionism; unlike the Baltic states, these countries did not become states *within* the Soviet federation. And that makes them less susceptible to Russian expansionism than the Balts.

Nevertheless, they are still weak and vulnerable, both politically and economically, and they often feel threatened. Within NATO and the EU, they tend to look to the United States for protection and less so to the Western European countries. This tendency has produced a split in Europe between the West and the East; it has also given the United States a group of Eastern allies within NATO and the EU that are often more loyal than the historic allies located in the West.

The United States obviously wants to maintain Eastern Europe as a democratic, free, independent, and economically successful zone. The United States also likes the idea of Eastern Europe as a wide buffer between Russia and the West. At the same time, Russia remains a preoccupation in Eastern Europe because of its size, proximity, large army, and the gas and oil that it sometimes uses to pressure East European governments. Presently, Russia is also weak economically and strategically; probably both the United States and Eastern Europe prefer to keep it that way.

Southeast Europe: The Balkans

When you enter the Balkans in Southeast Europe, you enter a different world. Are the Balkan countries part of Europe or not? Sometimes it is hard to tell. Geographically this area is part of Europe, but culturally, socially, religiously, and economically it is only partially and incompletely Western and European.

We need to make some distinctions here. Greece is a Balkan country, but it has been a member of the EU and NATO for a long time and, while Greece has its own culture and, often, its own way of doing things, it is definitely a Western and a very civilized country. Slovenia, once part of Yugoslavia, is a Catholic country, along with Greece the wealthiest of the Balkan countries, a full member since 2004 of both the EU and NATO, and also can be considered fully Western. Romania and Bulgaria were also admitted to the EU and NATO, not because they were qualified but because the United States during the Iraq and Afghanistan wars wanted access to military bases there. Of the two, Romania is the most Western in language, religion, and culture; but it is also very poor, very corrupt, and not fully integrated into Western ways, including democracy and a modern economy. Bulgaria is similarly corrupt and culturally, religiously, and historically close to Russia; it is conceivable that Bulgaria may fall back into Russian hands.

Now we get to the really tough cases. Serbia, which was the chief culprit in the bloody Balkan civil wars and genocides of the 1990s, is a candidate for EU and NATO membership; but it also has a strong pro-Russia faction and culturally, religiously, linguistically, and ethically it is often closer to Russia than to the West. Albania is a Muslim-majority country and very corrupt, but as a small country, it may be admitted to the EU and NATO as a way of demonstrating these institutions are not anti-Muslim—especially important if big (and Muslim) Turkey is not admitted. Bosnia and Kosovo are poor, majority-Muslim, violent, and may burst into civil war; they might conceivably be admitted to the EU and NATO as a way of pacifying them. Macedonia is another small, landlocked Balkan state; it, too, wants to join Europe's two great clubs but is locked in a conflict with Greece over its name (which is also a province in Greece) and other matters.

As you cross the mountains into the Balkans, you encounter a world that you can hardly believe still exists in Europe. First, the poverty, malnutrition, and illiteracy are great. Second, social conditions are often closer to the Third World than to the First or Second. Third, the politics are often tribal, patronal, and clan-based rather than national. In rural areas, cut off for centuries from Western civilization, there are still stories of witches, werewolves, and strange sex habits—Dracula was from this region. The Cyrillic alphabet is often used rather than the Western one; local dialects are often unintelligible to outsiders.

A thousand years ago, from Constantinople (now Istanbul), many of these areas were converted to the Orthodox religion, which is Eastern and closer to Moscow than it is to the Western religions, either Catholic or Protestant. Then, for some five hundred years in some parts, the Balkans were overrun by the Ottoman Turks and converted to Islam, which explains why Albania, Bosnia, and Kosovo are Muslim-majority countries even today. By language, alphabet, religion, culture, history, sociology, and politics, many parts of the Balkans are closer to the East, even the Middle East, and fit only uncomfortably into the West.

So can the Balkans be considered a part of Europe or are they more accurately seen as apart from it? It is a close call. Metternich, the great German statesman, used to refer to this area as "beyond the pale"—meaning beyond the pale of Western civilization. And Austrians, when asked where Europe ends, only half-jokingly respond,

"Somewhere southeast of Vienna"—meaning in the Balkans. For here is where violence is widespread; ancient hatreds and feuds dominate the landscape; and where Europe in the early 1990s was reluctant to go to quell civil war and genocide, thinking that this area was "not fully European" and leaving the United States to do this "dirty work" for them.

Obviously, the United States would like to see a peaceful, stable, economically prosperous, democratic Balkans. But given the low level of economic development, the weak infrastructure, and the violent and clan-based culture of the region, those goals are unlikely to be accomplished soon. Meantime, who is responsible for this area—we or the Europeans? Frankly, we have few interests there; as former secretary of state James Baker once unfortunately but memorably put it, "We don't have a dog in this fight." The United States only became involved because the Europeans, who also have strong doubts if this area is really European, failed to act, and because the genocide practiced there and shown nightly on U.S. TV made it impossible *not* to act.

So here we have another one of those areas where the United States has only limited interests at stake, which really should be the responsibility of the Europeans, but which becomes our "kettle of fish" because no one else *will* act. Nevertheless, the issues remain: is the Balkans part of the West and of Europe or not, whose responsibility is it, and if we don't assist it and integrate it (essentially) into the EU and NATO, might not parts of it (Bulgaria and Serbia) join forces once again with Russia, while other parts (Albania, Bosnia, and Kosovo) possibly become havens for Islamic fundamentalism and terrorism?

Even Farther East: Into the Former Soviet Union

After I'd completed my study of EU and NATO enlargement in 2001,[4] I'd pretty much concluded that was where Europe "ended": with the Baltic states and then following a line from the Baltic down to the Black Sea. It thus included all the countries—Poland, Czech Republic, Hungary, Slovakia, Romania, Bulgaria, Slovenia—discussed so far but nothing to the east of that.

Since then, however, we have had the Orange Revolution in the Ukraine and the Rose Revolution in Georgia. Belarus is still under an old-style, Moscow-oriented dictator but there are stirrings of democracy even there. Moldova has had democratic elections that resulted initially in an old-line communist party coming back into power, and more recently a pro-Western alliance. Democracy is insecure, incomplete, and nonconsolidated in these countries but, to varying degrees, all of them aspire to a democratic outcome. Armenia and Azerbaijan have also become independent nations.

With democracy has come a strong drive to join the EU, or at least to take advantage of the EU's trade and investment possibilities because in all these countries the EU is associated with wealth, prosperity, and affluence.

NATO is a different matter. The Ukraine and Georgia would love to join NATO because they see it as offering them U.S. military protection from a resurgent and possibly aggressive Russia. Belarus, however, at least for now, sees its future as tied to Moscow, while Moldova, with its uncertain leadership, is less sure about NATO and likewise does not want to antagonize Russia by joining the West. Both the Ukraine and Georgia, nevertheless, have taken some of the preliminary steps in preparation for joining NATO, though full membership may be a long way off. The United States tends to favor membership for these nations (bases en route to Iraq and Afghanistan, a tightened security perimeter around Russia), while our European allies are wary: first, because they see it as prohibitively expensive and second, because they are more fearful of antagonizing Russia. But the question always is: Can you have the economic benefits of joining the EU without also having to assume the security responsibilities implied in NATO membership?

If these countries continue on a democratic path, continue to make reforms in their government and economy, and *want* to join the EU and NATO, what is to stop them? That is a tricky issue. Because once a country begins the EU/NATO membership process, the record so far is that no one gets turned down. First, there is momentum; second, there are the strategic needs that often overwhelm other considerations; and third, once you put a country through all the hoops of the membership requirements *and* the country complies, then you no longer have a basis for saying no. And to say no at that late stage would likely be so destabilizing to the country involved that it would be completely self-defeating.

So why not just go ahead and bring them into the EU/NATO fold? Here, too, the going gets tricky—although it is sometimes a sensitive matter to the nations affected even to talk about these issues. But there are also strong reasons for *not* admitting these newest candidates:

1. Look at table 3.1 again: Georgia, the Ukraine, Armenia, Azerbaijan, Belarus, and Moldova are the poorest nations on the list by far. Remember our dictum: the farther east you go, the poorer it gets. It would take truly massive subsidies from the other European countries, on top of huge subsidies already committed to modernize the rest of Eastern Europe, to bring these newest candidates up to even minimal levels. And European taxpayers do not want to pay more than they already do to accomplish this goal.

2. These, or at least Belarus and Ukraine, are very big and populous countries. At this stage, it is easier for the EU and NATO to absorb small countries (Albania, Croatia) than big, populous ones. With the latter, the costs and difficulties are much higher.

3. These countries, unlike the rest of Eastern Europe, were long (for hundreds of years) an integral part of Russia and of the Russian federation. They still have strong ties to Russia and many of their people speak Russian. They look as much to Russia for protection as to the West.

4. There are important cultural differences between the West and the East here in terms of language, religion, alphabet, and political tradition. These obstacles are not impossible to overcome, but they are difficult.

5. Another reason the Europeans are wary of bringing Moldova, Belarus, the Ukraine, Armenia, Azerbaijan, and Georgia in is that these countries lie perilously close to what the Europeans see as potential instability, conflict, and, therefore, trouble for them. These trouble spots include Iran, Iraq, Afghanistan, Central Asia, the Caucasus, and, in general, the Muslim or Middle Eastern world. Europe fears that admitting some of these far-to-the-east nations (all of those mentioned earlier are Eastern Orthodox Christian except Azerbaijan, which is majority-Muslim) will inevitably, and at great expense to it,

suck Europe into these conflicts to which it would much prefer not to be a party.

6. Russia is wholeheartedly against any further expansion of the EU and NATO. It was not happy with the earlier enlargement into Eastern Europe, but these have a history as independent countries and Russia could live with that. But these others—Georgia, Belarus, Moldova, Armenia, Azerbaijan, the Ukraine—it views as part of *its* historic, national, Great Russian territories. And if not any longer its territories, then certainly within its sphere of influence, into which the United States and NATO should not intrude. The Europeans, especially, are sympathetic to the Russian point of view on this issue.

7. Finally, it should be said that public opinion in these countries is by no means unanimous on the issue of joining the EU and NATO. Moldova, recall, had until recently a communist government and Belarus is still linked closely to Moscow. Georgia, even farther east in the Caucasus, wants U.S. and NATO protection for its independence; but it has already lost part of its territory to a Russian incursion into South Ossetia (which Georgia also claims); it is extremely vulnerable to the nearby Russian army, and public opinion in Georgia prefers an accord with Russia rather than more confrontations. Armenia and Azerbaijan are both small countries, but they are important either for the oil they possess (Azerbaijan) or for the fact that vital oil pipelines cross their territory (Armenia).

An interesting feature of both the bigger and more important countries of Belarus and the Ukraine is that, because of the aforementioned one-time Polish-Lithuanian Empire, the westernmost provinces of these two countries tend to be Catholic rather than Orthodox, oriented toward the west culturally and economically, and much more favorable to the EU and NATO than those countries' eastern provinces. So here we have a situation where the "civilizational divide" (Samuel Huntington's term[5]) runs not along national borders, which makes things relatively easy, but *through* the interior of these countries, which makes things very complex. In other words, Belarus west of Minsk and the Ukraine west of Kiev are basically Western, while Belarus east of Minsk and the Ukraine east of Kiev are oriented toward Moscow. That makes things very complicated.

So in the end we leave it to our readers: Should Moldova, Belarus, the Ukraine, Armenia, Azerbaijan, and Georgia come into the EU, NATO, and the Western family of democratic nations or not? Or should some of these (but which ones?) come in and others not? Another alternative generally favored by the European countries is some kind of associated states within the EU and NATO but not full membership. However, this is generally opposed by these eastern countries themselves as implying "second-class citizenship": they want full membership or none at all. So what say you, dear reader: up or down, in or out?

One final issue needs to be mentioned here, and that is the status of Russia itself. During the 1990s, after the fall of the Soviet regime and when people were still hopeful about Russia's democratic and developmental prospects, there was considerable talk of bringing Russia, eventually, into the EU and perhaps even NATO. Some preliminary steps were even taken in that direction: Russia had a mission and "observer" status at NATO headquarters in Brussels.

Russia is, of course, the world's largest nation in territory and the eighth largest in population, so bringing them in would be a difficult task, but not an impossible one. However, since then Russia has gone back to more authoritarian ways under Vladimir Putin, it has turned more aggressive toward its neighbors, and the Russian government has made it clear it wants no part of NATO, even viewing it as "the enemy." It has a different attitude toward the EU, which it sees not like NATO as a military alliance threatening Russia but as a source of investment funds for its growth. Here the problem is, however, that the present EU countries see Russia as terribly corrupt, not a good investment risk, and too big and too poor for future EU membership.

On the other hand, it may be that a post-Putin or successor Russian government may come to see the West, the United States, and NATO in a more positive and nonthreatening light. Then the question of Russia's possible membership in the EU and NATO will undoubtedly come up again. We take up the issue in more detail in the next chapter; but if we are already thinking about the eastward expansion of Europe and the question of where Europe ends, then at some point Russia will have to come into the discussion.

Conclusion

Eastern Europe was long considered to be on the periphery of Europe. It was far poorer than the core area of Europe, less modern, less developed, having missed out on all the great modernizing movements of Europe that we associate since the sixteenth century with the making of the modern world. Not only was Eastern Europe poor and underdeveloped but these weaknesses made it susceptible to the pressures and military conquests of surrounding and more powerful neighbors: Germany, Russia, Austria, and the Ottoman Empire. There were long periods when Eastern Europe all but disappeared under the onslaught of these foreign conquests, of which the long Cold War occupation by the Soviet Union was only the most recent.

Most of us cheered when Eastern Europe became free and democratic for the first time in fifty years following the collapse of the USSR in 1991. Seeking the affluence that is associated with Western Europe as well as protection from what they believed would be a revived and newly aggressive Russian bear, all the Eastern European states sought membership in the EU and NATO. On balance, the admission of the Baltic states and Central Europe plus Slovenia to these two great European clubs has been successful. Bulgaria's and Romania's admission has been less successful, while, with the exception of Croatia, the admission of Albania and the states of the former Yugoslavia remain problematic.

Any further admissions any farther east than that is even more difficult. Historically, Belarus, the Ukraine, Moldova, and Georgia were not a part of Europe. Closer to Russia than to the West, their politics, culture, societies, and economies are all pulled more toward the East than toward the West. If these countries are ever to join the West, it will have to be slowly and incrementally. There are just too many problems here for the West to take on, certainly not all at once. All of these reservations apply in spades to big, populous, unsettled Russia.

The problems here are essentially three. First, the countries of Eastern Europe and those that were once part of the Soviet Union are woefully poor and underdeveloped by Western Standards. They are "Second World" by the definition introduced here and will require many decades and massive subsidies to catch up. Second, these countries culturally are only partially and incompletely Western. By language, religion, alphabet, culture, sociology, and politics they are separate from the West and may never be fully assimilated into it. Third, and strategically, the farther east or southeast that the EU and NATO go in their enlargements, the more they are likely to run up against other states and territories that are both large and hostile: Russia and the Islamic world. From the Western point of view, why invite this kind of clash, why precipitate unnecessarily an unwanted and unwinnable "clash of civilizations," in Huntington's terms? At best, therefore, any future enlargement of the EU and NATO will have to proceed gradually, over time, and allowing for major adjustments on all sides. This process may take decades or more, but gradualism in a context of danger and potential conflict is not a bad policy.

Notes

1. Irving Louis Horowitz, *Three Worlds of Development* (New York: Oxford University Press, 1971).
2. Truth in advertising: through his think tank, the Center for Strategic and International Studies (CSIS), the author was involved in many of these activities, both as a consultant in Eastern Europe to help improve governance and civil society and as a participant in CSIS's efforts to mobilize the ethnic communities in support of European enlargement to the East.
3. Until 1955 the Soviet Union occupied approximately 20 percent of Austria. After 1955 the Soviets left but Austria was obliged to remain neutral and not join NATO as a condition.
4. Howard J. Wiarda, *Arriving at the End Game: The Politics of EU and NATO Enlargement* (Vienna: Austria Institute for International Affairs, 2002); also published as a special edition of *World Affairs*, 164 (Spring 2002).
5. Samuel P. Huntington, *The Clash of Civilizations and the Remaking of World Order* (New York: Simon and Schuster, 1996).

Suggested Readings

Biscop, Suen and John Lembke (eds.). *EU Enlargement and the Transatlantic Alliance* (Boulder, CO: Lynne Reinner, 2008).

Grayson, George. *Strange Bedfellows: NATO Marches East* (Lanham, MD: University Press of America, 1999).

Hansen, Birthe and Bertel Heurlin (eds.). *The Baltic States in World Politics* (Surrey, UK: Curazon Press, 1998).

Heuberger, Valerie et al. *At the Crossroas: The Yugoslav Successor States in the 1990s* (Frankfurt, GE: Peter Lang, 1999).

Howard, Marc M. *The Weakness of Civil Society in Post-Communist Europe* (Cambridge, UK: Cambridge University Press, 2003).

Johnson, Lonnie. *Central Europe* (New York: Oxford University Press, 2002).

Michta, Andrew. *The Limits of Alliance: The U.S., NATO, and the EU in North and Central Europe* (Lanham, MD: Rowman and Littlefield, 2006).

Neuhold, Hanspeter et al. *Political and Economic Transformation in East Central Europe* (Boulder, CO: Westview Press, 1995).

Simon, Jeffrey. *NATO Enlargement and Central Europe* (Washington, D.C.: National Defense University Press, 1996).

———. *NATO Enlargement: Opinions and Options* (Washington, D.C.: National Defense University Press, 1995).

——— (ed.). *NATO: The Challenge of Change* (Washington, D.C.: National Defense University Press, 1993).

Tismaneanu, Vladimir. *The Crisis of Marxist Ideology in Eastern Europe* (London: Routledge, 1988).

Wiarda, Howard J. *Where Does Europe End? The Politics of EU and NATO Enlargement* (Vienna: Austrian Institute for International Affairs, 2002).

CHAPTER 4

Russia

Russia, formerly the Soviet Union, is the world's largest country in terms of territory and the eighth largest (behind, in order, China, India, the United States, Indonesia, Brazil, Bangladesh, and Pakistan) in population. But it is only, despite its size, resources, and population, the twelfth largest country (behind, in order, the United States, China, Japan, Germany, Great Britain, France, Italy, Spain, Canada, Brazil, and India) in terms of gross national income (GNI). And yet Russia is usually included in the group of eight modern, developed countries, whereas Brazil and India, which outrank it, are not. Is there a double standard here? Of course, there is. More on this later.

Russia's population was listed at 142 million in 2007, but it is shrinking. This is due to three reasons. First, since the collapse of the Soviet Union in 1991, Russia has been deprived of those regions that have since become independent—precisely those countries discussed in the last chapter: the three Baltic states, Belarus, the Ukraine, Moldova, Georgia, Armenia, Azerbaijan, and Central Asia. The separation of these countries from Russia has halved its population.

Second, over a long period but especially since 1991, health standards in Russia have declined disastrously, resulting in an equally disastrous decline in life expectancy. Female life expectancy is considerably below European standards at seventy-three years, but male life expectancy has dipped to a precarious fifty-nine, nearly the same as that in countries like Sudan or Togo. These are Third World numbers, not

First or Second World ones. The reasons for this astounding decline for men are various: poor health standards and care, poor diet, lack of jobs and hope, widespread alcoholism, and depression from the Soviet Union's fall from superpower status. Russia has not yet adjusted to the fact that it is a *former* great power.

The third reason for declining population is lower birth rates. Russian women are having fewer children; Russia has one of the lowest fertility rates in the world. It is likely the low fertility is related to the aforementioned factors: declining health standards and facilities, diet, and alcoholism and related diseases among the men.

Russia's GNI is listed as $7,560 per person per year, and its purchasing power parity GNI at $14,000. The latter figure is merely an estimate; the first number is most accurate. That puts Russia at about two-thirds the level of the East European countries that were discussed in the previous chapter and admitted to the EU and NATO, and at about a quarter the living standard of Western Europe. It also puts Russia below the levels of Turkey and Mexico.

Russia is definitely not a First World (modern, developed, democratic) country. In the previous chapter we discussed why Russia and the Eastern European countries previously under its domination are not Second World, in the classic sense (developed but communist), either. Russia is nowhere near being a modern, developed country. There are many parts of Russia that are closer to Third World levels, where you see malnutrition, malnutrition-related disease, and woefully inadequate health care. At best what we can say is that Russia is an aspiring Second World country under our new definition: that is, it is *trying* to make it to the level of the wealthier Eastern Europe countries but it lacks infrastructure; its government and bureaucracy are severely dysfunctional; its democracy (if it can even be called that) is weak and unconsolidated; and its economy, relying almost exclusively on oil and natural gas, is fragile.

Russia may have, for the most part, left the Third World, but it is nowhere near First World status. We used the term "Second World" in its revisionist form to describe countries in transition from Third to First World but seemingly stuck in-between, perhaps indefinitely. Even if we grant Russia that Second World designation, we must recognize that it is at the lower end of that category, considerably below its neighbors (and former satellites—Poland, Hungary, etc.) in

Eastern Europe. Russia is low on our development scale and without oil or natural gas it would be sinking even further.

And yet, and yet... Russia is still a former superpower. As a legacy of that era it still has thousands of nuclear weapons along with the intercontinental ballistic missiles capable of delivering them. There is some question whether these weapons and missiles, in today's chaotic, disorganized Russia, actually work or are functional; but if only a few of them get through, that may be harmful enough. Plus, Russia has a large conventional army, a huge arms industry, immense resources, and all that oil and gas. We need, therefore, to be wary of Russia. Russia can be a troublemaker, a disruptive force in NATO and the EU, able to put enormous pressure on its East European neighbors and, through its oil and gas "diplomacy," on Western Europe as well.

Under Vladimir Putin, especially, Russia seems to be moving back toward authoritarianism. It has clamped down on the press and other freedoms; democracy is hanging by a thread; and human rights and the rule of law are regularly violated. The Russian secret police (Putin's background was in the old KGB, the Russian intelligence service) is being revived and the Russian army is being modernized and expanded. Under Putin, Russian nationalism is being revived; Russia is making aggressive moves toward its neighbors; and it is threatening Belarus, Moldova, the Ukraine, and Georgia (even invading the latter) if they make noises about joining NATO or allying with the United States, both of which Russia sees as a threat compared to the cooperative attitude of a decade ago.

So, we have a problem to deal with. The Russia of today is not the happy, cooperative, democracy-aspiring, free market–oriented country of a few years ago. It has turned ugly, belligerent, uncooperative, and aggressive. Does this mean we have a new Cold War on our hands? Must we be tough with Russia or try to accommodate it? Do we still try to promote democracy and free-market capitalism there or in the present circumstances do we give up, at least temporarily, on those goals? Should our policy be, as during the Cold War, containment of Russia, or an effort to bring it into the "civilizing" missions of the EU and NATO? And if the latter, what if Russia rebuffs our efforts?

There are lots of issues, problems, and potential conflicts with Russia. And all these are coming up when the United States already has its hands full with China, North Korea, Iran, Iraq, Afghanistan, India, Pakistan, Mexico, Israel, and other countries, to say nothing of our severe economic downturn. Surely the Russians know we are preoccupied and even bogged down in these other areas, which is one reason they think that in this context they can advance their interests at the U.S. expense.

Let us provide the background that enables us to understand Russia more fully.

Background

Russia has a long background as an underdeveloped area. And because of that, a long history of complex relations with the much more developed Western Europe. At some levels, Russia wants to be modern, developed, and civilized like the West, and integrated into Western ways and institutions; but at other levels it wants to go its own way, thumb its nose at the West, and be a power and a civilization (Slavic, Orthodox, both European and Asian) unto itself.

Russia is a vast, often primitive, cold, and frequently forbidding land. It encompasses both European Russia to the west of the Ural Mountains (and including Moscow and Saint Petersburg) and Asian Russia (including the vastness of Siberia) to the east of the Urals. Russia is immensely proud that it covers vast areas of both Europe and Asia and would not want to give any of it up. It traverses seven time zones versus three for the United States. I once asked a Russian taxi driver, just for the fun of it, how long it would take him to drive completely across his country. Thinking that it would take me anywhere from three to five days to drive across the United States, my taxi driver's response was eighteen days to cross Russia. Only part of that time difference could be accounted for by Russia's bad roads.

One needs to think of Russia like other vast, frontier societies: Canada, Australia, China, Brazil, and the United States itself. In all these countries, much of national history is taken up with the effort to subdue, pacify, and eventually civilize (we called this "Manifest Destiny") far-flung and distant frontier areas, to bring law and order to previously lawless and quite primitive regions. In the United States, Canada, and Australia this process is by now largely complete; in Brazil, China, and Russia it is still unfolding. And out on these frontiers, violence, disorganization, and lawlessness frequently accompany the process.

In Russia, as well as in some of the other countries named, this process has occurred mainly under authoritarian auspices. *Never* in Russian history has there been a democratic government capable of accomplishing these tasks; that is, of expanding and consolidating Russia's frontier, holding the country together, and stimulating development. In the grand sweep of Russian history from the twelfth century to today, the only successful governments have been strong, tough, authoritarian, often brutal governments. Think of Ivan the Terrible, Peter the Great, Catherine the Great, the czars, the communists, Stalin, Brezhnev, and now Putin. In the Russian psyche, development, growth, and national success have been associated with strong, authoritarian regimes, while paralysis, weakness, and failure are associated with Russia's usually brief and unhappy democratic experiences.

Russia's frontiers have been on three sides, actually four if we count the Arctic Circle. In the West, Russia's goals have long been to expand and secure its borders, establish a buffer (Eastern Europe) between itself and possible invaders (France, Germany), and find an all-year or warm-water port for its navy. To the east in Asian Russia, Russia has long sought to fill the vast empty spaces of Siberia, protect its rich natural resources, and ward off possible Chinese or Japanese incursions. In the south, Russia looks for secure borders, a defensive perimeter of allied states, and guarantees against rebellion by Russia's own sizable Muslim minorities. Up north, Russia maintains a cold-water navy and has recently, by submarine, planted its flag underneath the North Pole. These are all traditional, Great-Russian interests; there is nothing in President Putin's recent moves that is not in accord with these historic objectives.

While Russia has long had these external frontiers on its perimeter, it also has an internal "frontier." And that involves Russian poverty, backwardness, and the widespread desire to develop the nation. Read Dostoyevsky and especially Tolstoy to understand this internal frontier historically. For Russia has, by comparison with Western or even Eastern Europe, long been plagued by underdevelopment. Here the great enemies have been illiteracy, disease, chaos, disorganization, government and political ineptitude, and the omnipresent problem of alcoholism. And the way to solve these problems, Russians believe, can only come through strong government: the czars, the communists, now Putin. The struggle against underdevelopment and to achieve parity with the Western (and now also Asian) countries is an ever-present one in Russian history.

For here you have a large country, the world's largest, with immense natural resources—not just oil and gas, but also timber, coal, iron ore, manganese, just about everything. The problem in Russian history, continuing to today, is how to organize this large, disorganized, and chaotic country, to harness all those resources, and to achieve national development. No government in Russian's past, except maybe Stalin and the communists for a time, and now Mr. Putin, has ever been able to achieve the goal of disciplining and organizing the country for truly national development. To the degree that Putin is succeeding in doing that, he will enjoy immense popular support.

Under the czars, Russia remained a disorganized, chaotic country. Only under the last of the czars, especially Alexander II and Nikolaus II, did the country begin to modernize and develop, but that came too late and in 1917 the czarist regime was overthrown in revolution. It then took the communists some fifteen years to pacify, discipline, and reorganize the country; under Stalin in the 1930s, the country began large-scale industrialization and economic take-off. It was long said by apologists for the regime that, yes, Russia had few freedoms but at least Stalin industrialized and developed the country. True, but only up to a point. For while Stalin's totalitarian techniques succeeded in achieving initial industrialization, such a rigid and top-down system proved incapable of adapting to the requirements of a more modern economy based on advanced technology, computers, and electronics. After an initial spurt in the 1930s, 1940s, and 1950s, by the 1960s and 1970s Russia was falling further and further behind—behind not just the West but now the East (Japan, South Korea, Taiwan, Hong Kong, Singapore, and China) as well.

By the 1970s and 1980s, cracks were beginning to appear in the Soviet monolith, both in the economy and the political system. First, Russia was more socially pluralist than it had been previously; there wasn't really an interest group struggle as in the United States but there was the beginning of more diverse interests in politics. Second, Mikhail Gorbachev's policies of *glasnost* and *perestroika* brought a new degree of hope, possibility, and even some initial openings toward greater freedom not seen in Russia previously. But third, the Russian economy was not performing well and had proven to be noncompetitive. Then when Ronald Reagan stepped up the pressure by expanding the American Defense Department budget, the Soviet Union could not keep up and was essentially spent into the ground.

In the 1980s my colleague Vladimir Tismaneanu and I predicted the collapse of the Soviet Union by focusing on what we called its six crises.[1] First was the crisis of the economy, as described earlier. Second was the crisis of ideology: no one even in Russia, or *especially* in Russia, believed the Marxist ideology anymore. Third was a crisis in society: between the elite and the masses, within the elite over the future of the country, and between the generations, with young people wanting the freedom to speak and travel without restrictions. Fourth was the crisis of a one-party state, woefully inefficient, and with no choices. Fifth was the crisis of morality: widespread corruption, special favoritism, drug use and, again, alcoholism. Finally, there was an international crisis: the USSR had no friends, was more and more isolated, and the satellites in Eastern Europe were already breaking away.

When all these crises came together in the 1989–1991 period, the Soviet regime quickly collapsed. Moreover, it imploded from within, not as many had feared through a nuclear Armageddon. In fact, the long Cold War ended without a shot being fired, thanks both to the Russian leadership as well as to the shrewd policies of President George H. W. Bush (Bush I).

U.S. Policies and Interests

For just about all of the Cold War, from the end of World War II until the final collapse of the Soviet Union in 1991, U.S. policy could be summed up in a single word: containment. The containment strategy was articulated by George W. Kennan, a U.S. diplomat and writer on foreign relations. Writing in 1947, Kennan went into the details of Russian/Soviet culture and society. Rather than a head-on and risky military confrontation with the Soviets, Kennan suggested a long-term policy of patience. We should not provoke the Russian "bear," he said, but instead hem it in and contain it within its present borders.

That would require a long-term policy of waiting, of preventing further Soviet incursions into Western Europe, Asia, or the Middle East, of waiting the Soviets out until their own internal social and political forces had exhausted themselves and/or led to charges in the Soviet regime. And that is precisely what happened: the Soviet Union collapsed under its own weight and inefficiency. But fortunately it collapsed not with a nuclear bang but with a whimper.

U.S. policy now switched from containment to the active promotion of democracy, human rights, and free markets (capitalism) in Russia. The logic, which the United States had used in other parts of the world, was that a democratic and capitalistic Russia would stimulate economic prosperity, give rise to a large middle class, keep the Russian population content and happy, and thus prevent future conflict and confrontation. Moreover, in pursuit of these large goals, the United States sought to integrate Russia more closely into Europe, possibly even into the EU and NATO, and thus remove the hostility tinged with envy and not a little inferiority complex with which Russia had long viewed the West. Russia, in short, was to be no longer an enemy and Cold War rival but a partner for peace, democracy, and development. Who could argue with those lofty goals?

The trouble was that the goals had little to do with the reality in Russia. The problems included that Russia had no training or background in democracy—no political parties besides the communists, no civil society, no traditions of trust or a loyal opposition; its economy verged on total breakdown; and its government was riddled with corruption, inefficiency, and patronage. Part of the problem also was that, because of Soviet totalitarianism, few Americans and others had ever traveled much beyond the two major cities of Moscow and Saint Petersburg. They mistook what was happening there, including greater freedom and liberalization, for what was happening in the rest of the country. In fact, nothing could be further from the truth. While Moscow and Saint Petersburg looked relatively prosperous, democratic, and even free (the so-called Moscow Spring), the rest of the country had changed little.

Out in the vast Russian countryside, where few Moscovites or foreign diplomats ever ventured, statues of the communist state's founder Lenin still graced every town square; the local communist party and its officials were still in charge; and the same old "sleepy" and inefficient communist bureaucrats who had run things forever were still running things. Meanwhile, factories were closing down because there was no longer a market for their products; the huge Russian state farms were running down and not producing; and government agencies were grinding to a halt because no one was paying them. The successor democratic government led by Boris Yeltsin had proclaimed that farm land was now up for private sale, but no one had any money to buy; there was no credit or ag extension; and the farm machinery was rusting from disuse. Yeltsin would issue a decree-law or the new Congress in Moscow would pass some legislation, but these had no affect whatsoever out in the hinterland. It is a problem familiar to scholars of Latin America and other Third World countries where the government may issue a decree but its writ is hardly heard outside of the capital city.

I was in Russia during this period of the early 1990s, traveled widely around the interior, and witnessed personally many of the features described here. First, Russia was not set up for international business: no international hotels, no international telephone services, no FAX machines, no ATMs, no computers, no banks, no financial institutions. Second, the infrastructure was weak or lacking: potholed roads, no interior airports, unreliable electricity, cars and trucks that wouldn't run. Third, the Russians I met had often fanciful and totally unrealistic (they'd never been abroad or heard of market surveys) ideas about what they could sell to whom: the manager of the submarine factory told me he had plans to convert his subs to commercial use, fill them with logs, and ship them under the North Pole to Canada. (See if you can think of six reasons why that would be unsuccessful!)

At local as well as federal levels the government, the police, and the bureaucracy were still under the control of communist party hacks who had no interest in reform. The universities and the school system were all but closed down. As more and more factories closed down, the unemployment rate was climbing to 30 or 40 percent. No one had any money; families were doubling and tripling up in apartments; and stores were running out of goods and foodstuffs. In my traveling about, I saw malnourishment, children with bloated bellies (not from too much food but from too little), and the diseased and malformed bodies that you see in Third World countries. When I visited Russia's nuclear centers, I found nuclear waste flowing directly into the town's

water supply and, though I'm not a medical doctor, widespread leuke-
mia due to radiation exposure.

Initially, the Russians had welcomed the Americans and others who
had come there postcommunism to help them forge a new way. My
assignment, brought in by the Russians, had been to help them set up
new university-based, non-Marxist departments of political science
and international affairs. For my troubles, I was roughed up a couple
of times by local communist officials who resented my presence and
message. The only other foreigner with me in Nizhny Novgorod,
Russia's third largest city, east of Moscow and on the banks of the
Volga River, was a Canadian geneticist there to teach the Russians
about breeding cows. The Swedes,[2] Germans, Austrians, Americans,
and others were bringing investment into Russia, but they soon pulled
out because (i) there was little money to be made in Russia and (ii) the
entire system was so corrupt that they could not function. Thereupon,
the European investors concentrated on Eastern Europe, which was
closer to home, had greater certainty of profits, and was less problematic in terms of corruption and other factors.

Eventually, I returned from the interior to Moscow and went to the
U.S. embassy to report on what I'd seen and experienced. The embassy
at that time was headed by Ambassador Robert Strauss, a personal
friend and a Washington wheeler-dealer. I reported that in my travels I saw *no* democracy and *no* free markets out there in the Russian
countryside. Mainly what I saw was chaos, disorganization, and collapse. But that is not the message the embassy wanted to hear. The
United States was *ideologically committed* to the democracy-capitalism
agenda—even if that did not exist in Russia. That was the only message the embassy's political and economic counselors wanted to hear.
They could not conceive of any other path for Russia. Had the United
States not been so committed to its own ideologically driven policy
and allowed for some truly Russian solutions to their own problems,
our relations with Russia would not be as sour as they are now.

Russia's Evolution

Russia has gone through two quite dramatic evolutions since the collapse of the Soviet Union in 1991. The first, in the early 1990s, involved
a quick, dramatic, but also short-lived changeover to democracy and

capitalism. Led by the mercurial (and alcoholic) Boris Yeltsin, Russia sought to transition almost overnight in the political sphere, from totalitarianism or its milder form of authoritarianism to democracy, and in the economic realm from communism to capitalism. As with all such large-scale transitions, this period was marked by a great deal of confusion, uncertainty, and chaos.

As a former communist country that had just decreed the end of communism, Russia totally lacked the institutions necessary for either democracy or private enterprise. It had no democratic political parties, no independent labor unions, no business or interest groups, no civil society, no parliament, no election machinery, no nothing. Nor, economically, did it have a stock market, banks, lending procedures, financial institutions, regulatory agencies, or a currency (the ruble) that was worth anything. Russia was, literally, one of those countries that had to start all over again from scratch. It had *zero* institutions on which to build either democracy or a free-market system. Moreover, because of its long isolation and the totalitarian nature of the Soviet regime, the Russian people as well as its leaders had no clear idea where to start.

Because of this lack, in the early months and years after communism's collapse, Russia warmly welcomed outside advice and expertise. It brought in economists, business advisers, political scientists, and many others to help it through the transition. Russia was at this time confused and uncertain about its destiny: the old system had collapsed but no new one had as yet emerged to replace it. The government and the Russian people were, therefore, warmly welcoming to outsiders (including me) who came to Russia to assist.

But then lots of things began to go wrong: the Russian "train" ran off the tracks. What were some of those changes?

First, Boris Yeltsin, who was earlier championed as the great apostle of democracy, riding on a tank to rally the Russian people and bravely defying Soviet authorities, proved to be totally incompetent as a president and government leader. Yeltsin, initially, had charisma, but he did not know how to govern or administer anything. He had bouts of depression, drank heavily to the extent of going on binges and disappearing for days or weeks at a time, and allowed corrupt cronies and family members to take advantage of his good nature. Toward the end of his rule, Yeltsin was no longer in control.

Second, in addition to the president, Russia lacked institutions that could help usher it through the transition. The parliament, elected in great hope, proved to be a den of corruption; when they watched it on TV (like C-Span), Russians found its antics, fights, and uninformed debates laughable. Nor did Russia have an efficient and functioning court system, police, or local government. Journalism was sensationalist and often ill-informed; the human rights situation soon deteriorated; and Russia became a very violent and corrupt country.

Third, the Russian economy went into a downward tailspin. As indicated, Russia lacked banks and other financial institutions; in addition, it had no idea how capitalism and free markets worked. Essentially, what happened is that the ailing, incompetent, and often out-of-it Yeltsin, himself not knowing what to do, allowed, and even encouraged, corrupt administrators, factory managers, and family members to take advantage of the system for private purposes. There followed one of the greatest rip-offs in all of history. With Yeltsin frequently blacked out and no effective controls or regulatory procedures in place, these cronies took advantage of the privatization decrees and their own insider knowledge to secure the former state-owned industries, as well as lucrative contracts, for themselves.

Virtually the entire patrimony of the Russian state, which was, of course, immense because in a communist system the state owned almost everything, was drained away into private, corrupt hands. And when I say the "entire patrimony," I mean everything: government ministries, offices, and vast state-owned enterprises were stripped of desks, typewriters, file cabinets, computers, telephones, even the wiring. This was the beginning of the so-called Russian oligarchy, a group of billionaires who got immensely rich by literally stealing everything in sight at a time when there was no or minimal supervision of their activities. There is a saying in the United States that behind every great family fortune is some kind of dirty or corrupt business deal; in Russia, this would be true in spades. These billionaires, in addition, wield immense power behind the scenes; without them, the entire Russian economy, already perilous, would collapse.

A fourth factor explaining what went wrong is that the international community, seeing all these bad things happening domestically in Russia, became disillusioned and pulled out. That included both the Europeans and the Americans. Foreign aid programs dwindled as they proved almost impossible to carry out in the vast Russian hinterland; even more important in terms of dollars lost, private foreign direct investment (FDI) began pulling out as well. These foreign firms found that Russia was so corrupt that there was no rule-of-law to protect them, and that they could not compete with the local oligarchs who not only had monopoly power and inside political connections but could even effectively bar the foreign firms from competing. After butting their heads against these walls for five or six years, most of these foreign investors simply gave up on Russia.

Meanwhile, by the late 1990s and on into the twenty-first century, important changes were also occurring in Russia itself. What are some of these features, which also help explain current Russian foreign policy?

1. Russia remains a very poor country. Outside of Moscow and Saint Petersburg, and even within these cities but outside of the main tourist areas, poverty is widespread. Little of the wealth from Russia's recent oil boom has trickled down to the countryside or poor urban areas. One still finds widespread disease, malnutrition, and inadequate health care in Russia. Russian life expectancy has plummeted disastrously, especially for men. Part of Russia's aspirations to become a superpower once again, or at least a country to be treated seriously, hinge on its efforts to relieve these conditions.

2. Going beyond poverty, Russia remains in many respects a Third World country. Or perhaps Second World—not in the older sense of a developed communist country but in the sense of a formerly communist country like Poland or Hungary that is *aiming for* development and modernization, hasn't completed that transition yet, and may be *permanently* locked in a less-developed or intermediary stage. In what we now term Second World countries, the government works only partially; the bureaucracy is ineffective and doesn't deliver much in the way of goods or services; corruption is widespread; national infrastructure is inadequate; and democracy is largely a façade.

3. Russia is becoming a one-crop economy. In this case, the "crop" is oil, accounting for up to 80 percent of Russia's foreign exchange. So long as oil prices are high, Russia, like Dubai, Saudi Arabia,

or Venezuela, prospers; but when oil goes down as happened recently, Russia can be quickly in trouble. Meanwhile, agriculture, manufacturing, and industry have all lagged, reflecting Russia's disintegration after the Cold War and its continuing Third or Second World problems.

4. The Russian state is increasingly authoritarian and top-down, reflecting both Russia's authoritarian past and the present weakness of democratic institutions and civil society. Russia has elections and, therefore, can be called an "electoral democracy," but not a liberal or a pluralist one; and once the elections are over, almost all power is delegated ("delegative democracy") to Prime Minister Putin with no democratic checks and balances. Rather like Hugo Chávez in Venezuela, there is widespread popular support in Russia for Putin-style authoritarianism as long as the economy continues to expand; but should the economy contract, and absent democratic safeguards, the Russian regime could quickly face grave difficulties. Meanwhile, there are few functioning institutions to deliver goods and services and hold it all together.

5. Russian nationalism is on the rise. Nationalism has many manifestations including newfound pride in Russian accomplishments (outer space, tennis, the squeeze on Georgia), anger at those (Gorbachev, Yeltsin) thought responsible for Russia's fall from great-power status, and increasing rejection of the West, Western ways, and those Western "clubs" (NATO, the EU) that Russia once seemed eager to join, and a reassertion of historic Russian institutions including the Orthodox Church, the military and the secret police (Putin's former institution), and even binge drinking.

6. Part of Russian nationalism involves rising anti-Americanism. Increasingly, Russians blame the United States (Presidents Bill Clinton and George Bush, Clinton's secretary of state Madeleine Albright, and such U.S. agencies as the National Endowment for Democracy—NED) for leading them in wrong (non-Russian) directions, taking advantage of them when they were weak, and expanding the U.S. security perimeter *inside* what they see as Russian national territory: the Baltics, Ukraine, Georgia, Central Asia. Certainly, when President Barack Obama visited

Russia in the summer of 2009, he got a much colder reception than he'd received in other parts of the world—no Obama mania here. Similarly, the welcome many Americans received in the early-to-mid-1990s, when Russia looked to the United States and U.S. institutions for inspiration, leadership, and guidance, is now gone.

7. Two comments should be made about Russia's changing political culture. First, there has been a reassertion of historic Russian political culture: religion in the most traditional forms is on the rise; there is a disturbing tolerance for authoritarian solutions; democracy is being denounced as a foreign import; and anti-Semitism, anti-Muslim, and anti-foreign sentiments—anything or anyone deemed "non-Russian"—are all, disturbingly, increasing.

Second, the popular mood in today's Russia is sour, angry, and bitter. Russia has long been a grumpy, boorish country, often fueled by one of the world's highest levels of alcohol consumption; but this is something new. Russians are truly angry—at the United States, at their own leaders—for their precipitous fall from superpower status. An angry, nationalistic, quasi-paranoid, newly aggressive Russia, like an angry Germany, is a condition we should seek to avoid.

Policy Implications

At several levels—poverty, disorganization, dysfunctionality—Russia is a Third World country. But it also has oil, natural gas, vast resources, and, thanks to various and ongoing crash programs, thousands of nuclear weapons, an intercontinental ballistic missile system capable of delivering at least some of those nukes, and a large conventional army equipped with tank battalions and thousands of armed personnel carriers. The Russian people may be deprived and at Second or Third World levels, but the armed forces are well-equipped and provided for—a First World military in a Third World country. To this impressive military might have now been added potent Russian nationalism, anger and bitterness toward the West and the United States in particular, and a newfound aggressiveness that seeks to reverse past losses.

In recent years Russia has pursued increasingly bellicose positions and actions:

- It is flexing its military muscle in Latin America, the Arctic, and the Black Sea.
- It has told the Ukraine, Moldova, and Georgia in no uncertain terms that it will not allow them to join NATO.
- It militarily invaded and "liberated" the former Georgian provinces of South Ossetia and Abkhazia as a way of teaching breakaway Georgia a lesson and securing greater Russian Black Sea access.
- It used its oil and natural gas to put political pressure on Belarus, the Ukraine, the Baltics, and much of Western Europe.
- It told the United States not to build its missile defense systems in Poland or the Czech Republic, which the United States says is aimed at Iran but Russia believes is directed toward them. It has also told these two countries not to allow the United States to put in its missile defenses on their soil. The United States then acquiesced to Russian demands.
- It has reduced its participation in EU and NATO activities and told these two clubs it does not want to be a member.
- It conducts provocative military exercises on the borders of the Baltic states, the Ukraine, and Georgia with the obvious intent of intimidating these countries.
- On such difficult issues as Iraq, Iran, Afghanistan, and North Korea, which require multilateral diplomacy to be successful, Russia has proved to be purposely uncooperative and unhelpful.
- Russia continues to make threatening and bellicose statements that frighten the Europeans especially, since they live closer to the Russian threat than we do, raising the spectacle of a new cold war and also serving to divide NATO and the EU.
- Russia has sent its military forces into the breakaway territory of Chechnya and brutally suppressed, with widespread human rights violations, the Chechnyan independence movement, which also happens to be Muslim. This message was aimed not just at the Chechnyans but also at other possible Muslim independence groups on Russia's southern borders.
- Russia now talks of a "sphere of influence" that includes the Baltics, Eastern Europe, parts of the Balkans, Belarus, the

Ukraine, Georgia, and Central Asia. It indicates the United States and NATO should keep their hands off and not be involved there, and certainly these countries and areas should not be a location for NATO bases or armies.

Recent Russian military incursions into Chechnyan, South Ossetia, Abkhazia, and Georgia are likely only a foretaste of what is to come, as Russia continues to flex its diplomatic and military might. Nor can Russia be expected to be very cooperative in international forums, to lend its cooperation to U.S. initiatives, or to accept its present status as a second-rate power.

Russia's goal is to restore its former superpower prestige and power. It can be expected to suppress any future breakaway or independence movements within its borders, to threaten its neighbors against joining NATO, and to use its oil and gas resources, to say nothing of widespread European anxiety about the Russian bear's intentions to extract concessions from the United States and from both Western and Eastern Europe. Bulgaria, Moldova, and the Ukraine are already falling back into (Belarus never left) the Russian orbit; other countries, such as the Baltics or Poland, may follow. Some European diplomats are already saying that they think it inevitable, given their proximity to Russia and the West's inability or unwillingness to respond, that the Baltic states of Estonia, Latvia, and Lithuania will be reoccupied one day by Russian forces.

What is to Be Done?

This is not the time for the United States, NATO, and the EU to be pushing for democracy promotion in Russia. We should *stand for* democracy, human rights, civil society, and reform, but the mood in Russia is not one in which major activist U.S. programs will be welcomed. At this time, Russia is too sensitive, too nationalistic, and too anti-American for such programs to be successful. The climate has changed from fifteen years ago when such U.S. initiatives were warmly welcomed. Now we must bide our time. In any case, we must recognize, as in Haiti, Iraq, or Afghanistan, that nation- and democracy-building efforts such as these will be projects of three or four *generations*, not three or four years as U.S. politicians often seem to believe. Do we have the funds and the political will for such a long-term commitment? Probably not.

The Barack Obama administration recognized these new and limiting realities when the president made his first visit to Russia in the summer of 2009. The agenda advanced by the administration included a resumption of strategic arms control talks, a reactivation of the moribund NATO-Russia Council, which had been suspended after Russia's invasion of Georgia in 2008, U.S. reconsideration of its plans to deploy a missile defense system in Eastern Europe, and (vague) offers of economic cooperation.

What can we say about this policy agenda? First, it is realistic, in the sense that it is a very limited agenda that recognizes the United States has, at present, little to offer Russia. Second, it is very modest and seems to involve the United States retreating on several fronts including missile defense and Georgia. Third, it is completely unimaginative: does anyone think a new round of arms control talks, after forty-plus years of such talks, even if successful, will fire the public's imagination? And fourth, it fails to address at all the key issues: Russia's need for economic development, for infrastructure growth, and for acceptability as a normal country in the family of nations. Surely we can do better than this very modest basis for policy.

Absent a more comprehensive policy, it is likely that we will face a more aggressive, nationalistic, and uncooperative Russia for some years to come. There will be pressure on *all* the new Eastern European countries, and especially those that were once an integral part of Russia itself: the Baltics, Belarus, Moldova, the Ukraine, Armenia, and Azerbaijan. Meanwhile, Russia will try to keep Europe off-balance and a little bit fearful of a renewed cold war, at the same time being uncooperative with and tweaking the United States at every opportunity. For example, in the summer of 2009, Russia granted over-flight permission to U.S. planes seeking to resupply our forces in Afghanistan from bases in Europe. Americans hailed this as a sign of renewed Russian cooperation, but the Russians saw it, slyly, as a way of sucking the United States deeper, like the Soviets themselves in the 1980s, into an unwinnable war in Afghanistan that could only be a drain on more of our resources.

The United States should continue to cooperate and work with Russia on as many levels and in as many policy arenas as possible. We need to collaborate with them and they with us. At the same time, through trade and investment, we need to help raise Russia up out of the Third World category and give it a rightful place in the world, if for no other reason than to remove Russia's gigantic inferiority complex and the various chips on its shoulders. That will, it is hoped, also help stabilize and moderate Russia's politics.

Meanwhile, we need to counter Russia's aggressive actions in the Baltics, Eastern Europe, and the Caucasus. It would be a stinging setback for the United States, to say nothing of the countries involved, if they were again subjected to Cold War–like pressures and intimidations stemming from Moscow or even, possibly, a military reoccupation. The United States, NATO, and the EU must all resist these Russian pressures and blackmail; there can be no Russian "sphere of influence" extended to these areas. But meanwhile, if Russia continues on its course of resurgence and aggressiveness, we should prepare for—dare we say it—a new round of Cold War–like containment. And in the present circumstances, containment would be much more complicated to enforce and carry out than before, both because the United States is now weaker financially and militarily than it was during the earlier Cold War *and* because other countries and regions—China, Japan, India, South Korea, Brazil, Germany, and the EU—are stronger and will take positions at variance with that of the United States.

As my Russian friends, recognizing the rising tensions on both sides and the near-impossibility of remaining positive about the future, said to me recently, with considerable irony, upon parting, "Stay optimistic!"

Notes

1. Vladimir Tismaneanu and Howard J. Wiarda (eds.), "The Vulnerabilities of Communist Regimes," special issue of *World Affairs* (Spring 1988).
2. The Swedes, in their self-important, not-always-lovable way, told us that Russia got socialism wrong (Stalinist) the first time, so they—the Swedes—would now help them get it right (social-democratic) the second time. Unfortunately, the Swedish efforts in these regards were no more successful than those of the other countries mentioned.

Suggested Readings

Broilard, Steve. *Russia in the Twenty-First Century* (Fort Worth: Harcourt Brace, 1998).

Cohen, Stephen. *Failed Crusade: America and the Tragedy of Post-Communist Russia* (New York: Norton, 2000).

Colton, Timothy. *The Dilemma of Reform in the Soviet Union* (New York: Council on Foreign Relations, 1986).

Dunlop, John. *The Rise and Fall of the Soviet Empire* (Princeton, NJ: Princeton University Press, 1993).

Nagy, Proska. *The Meltdown of the Russian State* (Cheltenham, UK: Edward Elgar, 2000).

Reddaway, Peter and Dmitri Glinski. *The Tragedy of Russia's Reforms* (Washington, D.C.: U.S. Institute of Peace, 2001).

Robinson, Neil (ed.). *Institutions and Political Change in Russia* (New York: St. Martin's, 2000).

Silverman, Bertram. *New Poor, New Russia* (Armonk, NY: M.E Sharpe, 2000).

Smith, Hedrick. *The New Russians* (New York: Random House, 1990).

Weigle, Marcia. *Russia's Liberal Project* (University Park, PA: Pennsylvania State University Press, 2000).

Wiarda, Howard J. and Vladimir Tismaneanu (eds.). "Vulnerabilities of Communist Regimes," Special issue of *World Affairs* (Spring 1988).

CHAPTER 5

Asia

Asia is today the most dynamic and growth-oriented area in the world. China is number two in the world (behind only the United States) in gross national income, and Japan is at number three. Other countries in Asia are growing rapidly as well, and Asia is fast becoming one of the key areas of international foreign relations. We are presently witnessing a massive reorientation in U.S. foreign policy away from Europe and toward Asia in recognition of these new realities.

The reasons for the rising importance of Asia are many:

1. It contains the world's two most populous nations (China and India) and five of the top seven (in order, China, India, the United States, Indonesia, Brazil, Pakistan, Bangladesh).
2. Asia has more nuclear powers than any other world area—China, India, Pakistan, Russia, and North Korea; possibly South Korea and Taiwan; quickly if it wished to, Japan.
3. In addition to Japan and China, other countries in Asia are growing rapidly—South Korea, Taiwan, Singapore, Hong Kong, Macao, now, in addition, Malaysia, Thailand, Indonesia, the Philippines, India, Pakistan, and Vietnam. *Several* of these countries—more on this later—are taking their place among the world's most dynamic economies.
4. There are, within Asia, some intense rivalries and competitions that may produce future—even nuclear—conflicts: India-Pakistan,

India-China, China-Japan, China-Taiwan, South versus North Korea, Japan-Russia, China-Russia, Indonesia-Singapore, Malaysia-Singapore, Vietnam-Laos, Vietnam-Cambodia, and Thailand-Myanmar. In fact, virtually every country in Asia has one or more actual or potentially dangerous conflicts brewing with its neighbors.

5. While Asia contains some of the world's richest nations, it also contains some of the world's poorest ones—Myanmar, Bangladesh, Laos, Cambodia, North Korea, East Timor—and, therefore, the potential not just for major power conflict but also for conflict *within* nations.

6. The world's power balance and geographic focus are shifting away from Europe and the West, more generally, and toward Asia. Everyone recognizes this but few talk about it publicly. Such a massive global power shift is bound to create tensions and discord (witness our own efforts to blame China for all our ills) both within the countries losing power and in and between those gaining it.

For these and other reasons, Asia has zoomed to the forefront in terms of American foreign policy priorities. It will likely stay there for a long time to come. Therefore, it behooves us to know far more than we do about Asian culture, languages, society, politics, and economics.

Socioeconomic Data

There is a long tradition in Western historiography and sociological thought—going back a hundred years to Max Weber and even longer in some cases—that suggested Asia would never develop in the same way the West had. Asia, it was said, strongly influenced by Confucius and the Confucian ethic, was too authoritarian, top-down, bureaucratic, hierarchical, and noninnovative to ever develop the entrepreneurial spirit for capitalism and growth to occur. But now we know the very Confucian values that earlier authors denigrated—its emphasis on order, discipline, organization, authority, honor (of parents and teachers), and, perhaps above all, education—are precisely the ones that enabled Asia to take off economically in the post–World War II period.

Japan was the first Asian nation to experience the takeoff and subsequent drive to maturity and economic wealth (see table 5.1).

Table 5.1   Asian per capita income

Country	Per capita income (in $)	Category
Australia	33,340	HIC
Bangladesh	1,341	LMC
Cambodia	1,690	LMC
China	5,370	UMC
East Timor	3,080	LMC
Hong Kong	44,050	HIC
India	2,740	LMC
Indonesia	3,580	LMC
Japan	34,800	HIC
Korea	24,750	HIC
Laos	1,940	LMC
Macao	20,000	HIC
Malaysia	13,570	HIC
Myanmar		LIC
New Zealand	26,340	HIC
Pakistan	2,570	LMC
Philippines	3,730	LMC
Singapore	48,520	HIC
Taiwan		HIC
Thailand	7,880	UMC
Vietnam	2,550	LML

HIC = High-income country (above $11,456); UMC = Upper-middle-income country ($3,706–11,456); LMC = Lower-middle-income country ($936–3,705).

Japan's industrialization began in the late nineteenth century after the Meiji Restoration of 1868; Japan quickly developed both light and heavy industry. Much of this industry was destroyed in World War II, but by the 1960s and 1970s Japan was on the way back. Some of Japan's products from this period—automobiles, for example, and other manufactured goods—were initially thought to be inferior, but by the 1980s Japan was manufacturing products—computers, sound systems, appliances, electronics, as well as automobiles—that were world-class and often better than those produced in the United States. Books began appearing that promoted "Japan as Number One," arguing that Japan's "Tiger Economy" would eventually surpass the

United States as the world's most productive economy. Japan was the first of many "Asian Tigers."

But during the 1990s and continuing to today, Japan went into an economic downturn from which it has still not fully recovered. Its per capita income has slipped in the last two decades from $44,000 per year (the world's richest) down to $34,600 (at the high end of the European average). Japan is still one of the wealthiest countries in the world with one of the world's highest living standards and life expectancies: eighty-six years for women, seventy-nine for men (tied for first place in the world). Moreover, one should not count Japan out: it remains one of the richest, most energetic, most orderly and disciplined, most organized, and ambitious nations on earth, certain to be a global leader far into the future.

Once the Japanese model was put in place and proved so successful (energy, hard work, discipline, organization, export-led growth), other countries—South Korea, Taiwan, Hong Kong, and Singapore, the four "Little Tigers"—were quick to follow. They closely followed the Japanese model, including the fact that some of their early products were of poor quality but over time acquired first-class rank—look at their computers, electronic devices, or the Kia automobile—and within a matter of three or four decades leapfrogged from Third World status to First World. The "Little Tigers" have by now joined Japan as among the most dynamic countries in the world.

South Korea and Taiwan were the first of the "Little Tigers" to take off in this way. Their per capita incomes are in the $25,000 per year range, which puts them above Portugal but below Spain and Italy, and still below the Western European average. Nevertheless, these two are still classified by the World Bank as "high-income" countries and are so dynamic and energetic that it would not be surprising if in the next decades they reach that wealthy, European average. Meanwhile, look at what has happened to the other two "Little Tigers," Hong Kong and Singapore: they have reached the mid-$40,000 per year per person level, which puts them above the rich West European average, equal to that of the United States, and behind only Luxembourg and Norway as the world's richest countries. Their wealth, as small city-states, comes not from industry or manufacturing but from commerce, business, shipping, trade, banking, insurance, and finance. If you want to see dynamism and energy in action, you have to experience Hong Kong and Singapore.

Most of us are aware of the economic takeoff of Japan, South Korea, Taiwan, Hong Kong, and Singapore, although we are probably not fully cognizant of the extent of their newfound wealth. When we consider that they all, particularly the "Little Tigers," began as poor countries only four or five decades ago, the extent and rate of their development in a relatively short period of time is truly remarkable. Most analysts refer to it as "miracle" economic growth.

What is now interesting—and not so well known—is that the Japan/"Little Tigers" model has recently spread beyond those five countries to other Asian countries as well. We may now include in that list such countries as Macao ($20,000 per capita), Malaysia ($13,570), Thailand ($7,880), and China ($5,370). We know about China's takeoff in the last two decades, but we are less likely to be as informed about these others. What is striking is that such heretofore laggard countries as Indonesia ($3,580 per capita income), the Philippines ($3,730), India ($2,740), Pakistan ($2,570—but before Pakistan was wracked by internal divisions), and Vietnam ($2,550) are beginning to get their acts together and to grow as well. Yes, this is the same Vietnam that was torn asunder by violence, civil war, revolution, and American military intervention in the 1960s and 1970s, but now united as a single nation and, similarly to these other countries, is on its way to economic growth.

That leaves Laos, Cambodia, Bangladesh, Myanmar, North Korea, and East Timor as the poorest of the Asian nations and not having begun the drive to takeoff yet. Moreover, we should not exaggerate the accomplishments of some of the others just listed. Malaysia, Thailand, China, Indonesia, the Philippines, India, Pakistan, and Vietnam are still poor countries. Though some of their recent gains have been impressive, they still lag *way behind* the "Tigers," still have large percentages of their populations in poverty, and still have a very long way to go. In both China and India, for example, because they have such large populations (over a billion in both cases), their gross national incomes are high, among the largest in the world (second place for China, twelfth for India). But on a *per capita* basis, neither country ranks very high and, despite recent impressive growth, is still classified as Third World rather than First World. Indeed, if one looks at the numbers closely, no more than 10–20 percent of the population in China or India are truly "making it" into the modern, developed world, while the rest of the population in these and the other poorer countries listed is still mired in poverty and Third Worldism.

Of such divisions between rich and poor are potential conflicts *within* nations made, to say nothing of the potential conflicts mentioned earlier *between* countries. While Asia is thus, at one level, the most dynamic area in the world, it is, at others, a region with a large potential for both intra- and interstate conflict.

History and Background

In much of Asia we are dealing with ancient cultures but relatively recent nation-states. In this sense, some of the countries of Asia—China, Japan, India, Vietnam, Cambodia, Malaysia, the Philippines, Indonesia—are like Iran, Iraq, Egypt, or Nigeria: *societies* and *cultures* that go back *thousands* of years but *nations* that are of relatively recent vintage. And with many of the problems familiar to new nations in Africa, the Caribbean, and the Middle East: setting boundaries, establishing the institutions of governance, determining legitimacy, separating the secular from the religious, defining the values and political culture of the nation, establishing effective control over often disparate territories, and achieving social and economic progress. In considering the difficulties of new nations, think of large China with its immense but diffuse population, India with its religious and ethnic differences, or Indonesia made up of thirteen thousand islands. In these three and other cases, the first nation-building task is to knit very diverse societies into a single nation-state.

One of the great mysteries that historians and social scientists continue to wrestle with is why China and India in the sixteenth and seventeenth centuries, with their already large populations, big national territories, and abundant natural resources, failed to keep pace with or even exceed the growth of Western Europe. From the sixteenth century on, it was "the West"—Spain, Portugal, Great Britain, Holland, France, eventually Germany and the United States—that came to dominate the world, not any of the Eastern or Asian states. The reasons for this probably have to do with technology (the industrial revolution and advances in weaponry), resources (abundant in Europe and

America, scarcer in Asia), culture (pragmatism vs. spiritualism), internal organization (unified at the national level, divided internally in Asia), and doubtless other factors as well. All this may now be changing as economic and, with it, military and political power shift away from Europe (and the United States as well?) and toward Asia.

During those centuries of what we in the West call the modern era, from the sixteenth century on, Asia fell further and further behind, while the West forged ahead. The Korean Peninsula remained mired in poverty and underdevelopment and was often the victim of either Chinese or Japanese aggression. Japan was torn by civil wars and rivalries among warlords (the S*hogun*) that for a long time hindered its development. Southeast Asia was similarly poor and undeveloped and was unable to forge the unity that would convert it into a major kingdom. China had unity and a central bureaucracy for a time, but it, too, degenerated into chaos and warlordism. India was a more religious society, but its very spiritualism, to say nothing of deep class, caste, religious, ethnic, and regional differences, prevented its emergence as a modern nation-state. *Nowhere* in Asia do we see parallels to what happened in Western Europe: the consolidation of the nation-state, the forging of national unity, and the drive to economic development.

As Europe moved ahead in the modern era and Asia fell further behind, another feature that further strengthened Europe's dominance and kept Asia down even longer was added: imperialism. As Western Europe became wealthier and more powerful, it also came to dominate Asia in imperialist fashion. First, the Spanish and Portuguese (principally the Philippines, India, China, Japan), then the Dutch (Indonesia, Japan), next the British (India and present-day Pakistan, the Malay Peninsula, Singapore, Hong Kong), then the French (Southeast Asia), and finally the Americans (Japan, the Philippines). Several of these combined to divide up China in the nineteenth-century opium wars, bringing the Middle Kingdom to an even lower level than previously. In *all* these cases, though in slightly varying degrees, imperialism meant the subjugation of Asia, the exploitation of its people and resources primarily for the benefit of the imperial countries, and the continued underdevelopment and subordination of Asia.

The first Asian country to break out of this syndrome was Japan in the last decades of the nineteenth century. Under the Meijee, Japan began to modernize, industrialize, and develop. By the end of the century, Japan was ready to take on Western power Russia in war and win; Japan also occupied and itself cruelly exploited parts of China and Korea. By the time of World War II (1938–1945), Japan felt strong enough militarily, politically, and economically to take on the United States and *almost* win, meanwhile conquering vast territories in China, Southeast Asia, Indonesia, the Philippines, and the South Pacific. Japan's rule in these areas was at least as cruel and exploitive as had been the earlier European imperialism and left a legacy of anti-Japanese sentiment throughout Asia that lingers to this day. Japan, meanwhile, in the post–World War II period, turned to internal development rather than external aggression and, as we know, was extremely successful at it. We shall have more to say about Japan's international position later in the chapter.

China, the other great East Asian country, had finally rid itself of most aspects of European imperialism, but it was plagued by continued warlordism and civil war and was unable to get its "act" together as a nation. The situation was extremely complicated because the European power, now plus Japan, continued to meddle in internal Chinese affairs, backing one or more warlords against another and keeping the country torn asunder. By the 1930s the situation had become even more complicated and violent with the emergence of a powerful communist movement in China under Mao Tse Dong. During World War II, the communists expanded their position ("The Long March"—to the west) even while Japan occupied much of eastern China. With the war ended and Japan driven out, the communists continued to make gains, eventually driving the Nationalist government led by Chang Kai Chek (supported by the United States) into exile on the island of Taiwan. Mao and the communists kept China in revolutionary turmoil for many years, but by the 1990s a more pragmatic (but still communist) leadership began the reform process that turned China into the economic dynamo and emerging global power that it is today.

The rest of Asia emerged as independent nation-states only after World War II. That means they have been independent for only fifty or sixty years, a relatively short time in the life of most countries, which is why we call them "new nations." India became independent in 1947; while India was primarily Hindu, Pakistan and

Bangladesh (once a part of Pakistan) were majority-Muslim. The Korean Peninsula, unlike these others never conquered by European imperialism, achieved independence after World War II as Japan was forced to withdraw and China was still exhausted by civil war; it was divided between a communist North and a Free-World South, and in the Korean War of 1950–1952 the two sides plus the United States on the side of the South locked horns in a brutal civil war. The Philippines had been an American colony since 1898; it achieved its independence in 1934 and achieved full sovereignty in 1946. The Dutch, also exhausted by World War II, could no longer hang on to Indonesia, which achieved its independence in 1949. Meanwhile, France, defeated by a communist uprising, pulled out of Indochina in the 1950s, leaving a legacy and a political vacuum into which the United States intervened in the 1960s (the Vietnam War) with disastrous consequences.

While all forms of imperialism are probably bad, it is important to remember that there were distinct forms of imperialism practiced by the different countries, with important consequences for today's Asian nations. Spanish and Portuguese legacies in the Philippines, India (Goa), China, Macao, Japan, and Taiwan are mainly of historical interest; though the Spanish and Portuguese left behind some aspects of their languages, religion, law, and culture, these influences—except in East Timor, a former Portuguese colony—are relatively unimportant today. British rule in India was often oppressive but it could also be benign and at least the British left behind a good educational system, a functioning bureaucracy, and a trained civil service to help India through its early independence years.

By contrast, the Dutch in Indonesia administered a cruel, slave-plantation system and never trained the Indonesians in self-government. Even today, sixty years later, knowledgeable Indonesians blame the Dutch for not establishing schools or a central bureaucracy capable of administering and holding the country together after the Dutch pulled out. France was probably the worst of the imperialist powers: it never did anything to develop Southeast Asia, precipitously pulled out after its defeat by the communists, and in effect dumped all the problems of the region into the arms of the United States. Finally, the United States: it often meant well and its policies were mostly benign, but it felt so superior to, so ethnocentric, and so patronizing, condescending, and even racist toward its wards (the Philippines) in Asia that its policies in the long run produced no better results than the other imperialists.

By the 1950s, by which time almost all these countries had achieved independence, the outlook for them was decidedly unpropitious. All of them were poor countries; none of them had developed industry; education lagged way behind; infrastructure was lacking; with the single exception of Japan, they belonged to the Third World rather than the First. So how did almost all of these countries, in the relatively brief fifty–sixty years since then, develop into the economic powerhouses that they are today? The "Asian Miracle" is one of the great success stories of the second half of the twentieth century.

While almost all of Asia now seems to be forging ahead, it is helpful to reflect on those countries of Asia that have been *most successful*. They are Japan, Singapore, South Korea, Taiwan, Hong Kong, Malaysia, Macao, China, and, slightly farther down the list, Vietnam. Think for a minute what all of these countries have in common: they were all shaped, going back many centuries, by the values, political culture, and organizational principles of Chinese/Confucian civilization. Even Japan, South Korea, Vietnam, and the others who today are rivals of, and seek to distinguish themselves from, China, owe much of their dynamic, hardworking, disciplined, and organized cultures to the impact of greater Chinese civilization. This point is important in its own right for understanding the emergence of these Asian countries as global world dynamos; but it may also point to something at least as important for international politics in the future: the reunification of these countries, or at least some of them, under the banners of Confucian culture and likely Chinese hegemony. That would make China a far greater global power than it is already in the process of becoming.[1]

U.S. Policies and Interests

The United States has a considerable history in Asia, going back to Commodore William Perry's visit to Japan in 1859. It has long seen Asia as a place for commerce, trade, and exports; since the Pacific was so wide, political and strategic interests came later.

Quite a bit of that history is inglorious, which is seldom forgotten in Asia though largely ignored in the United States. Consistently, the United States has treated Asia and Asians with condescension, a patronizing attitude, and racism. We called them "Yellow People" and worse, and were for a long time dismissive of their society and culture. In 1898 we conquered the Philippines and became its colonial master. In World War II we not only defeated Japan but also devastated its cities by bombing, including, in Hiroshima and Nagasaki, the only time nuclear weapons have ever been used in war.

We backed the wrong horse (Chang Kai Chek) in China, enabling the communists to take over the world's most populous country, which we then kept poor and isolated for the next thirty years. In the Korean War of 1950–1952, we turned back the communist invasion from the north but left the peninsula divided until today between North and South Korea. In the Vietnam War of the 1960s and 1970s, not only did we take the war to the communist North but we so devastated Vietnam and its neighboring countries, Cambodia and Laos, that we set back their development by forty years. Our repeated interventions and mucking around during the long Cold War in the internal affairs of the Philippines and Indonesia (remember Barack Obama lived in Indonesia as a boy during this period, an experience that strongly shaped his foreign policy views) have not endeared us to these two nations. Meanwhile, the United States has maintained a string of military bases, occupied territories, listening posts, and nuclear testing stations throughout the South Pacific that have often damaged these islands and led to bad relations between the locals and U.S. forces. Before we consider U.S. policy in the region, it is important to recall that the United States not only has a long history there but that in dealing with the region our hands are not entirely clean.

Here are the main U.S. policy interests in the Asian region:

1. We want an Asia that is politically stable, peaceful, and predictable.
2. We want an Asia that is open to American business, trade, commerce, and investment.
3. We want an Asia that has control of its nuclear and other weapons of mass destruction. Remember that Asia has more nuclear

states than any other world region, including such possibly irresponsible nuclear countries as North Korea and Pakistan.

4. We want an Asia that is economically prosperous, both because we want them to buy our products (think of a *billion*-plus possible consumers in both China and India) and because we believe a prosperous Asia is a stable Asia—our number one priority.

5. We want a democratic Asia that observes human rights, both for its own sake and because we believe that also adds to stability.

6. We want to strengthen Asian mutual security arrangements, through ASEAN and other institutions, so that Asia can solve its own disputes without dragging the United States into every conflict.

7. At the same time, the United States is seeking to work out bilateral treaties of cooperation, involving trade as well as security, with all the main countries of the area—Japan, South Korea, China, India, Pakistan, Indonesia, the Philippines, and Vietnam. In recent years this has been one of the more exciting areas of U.S. diplomacy and has opened up such countries as China and India to peaceful cooperation on numerous fronts.

Individual Countries

Now, as we did in other chapters, let us look at U.S. interaction in and relations with some of the key countries of the area.

Japan

Japan is the true "miracle economy" of Asia. Here we have a country of 128 million people (only the sixth most populous in Asia) on a string of relatively small islands, with almost no natural resources, and yet it is the third most productive in the world (behind only the United States and China) and a true wonder of efficiency and productivity.

How are we to explain Japan's remarkable success? First, the islands are unified culturally and socially; Japan has no large racial or ethnic minorities. Second, in the nineteenth century Japan achieved relatively centralized and efficient government earlier than the other Asian countries. Third, the Japanese are tremendously energetic, disciplined, organized, and hardworking; they *run* to work. Fourth, their industry is efficient and large scale; Japan is a fully industrialized country. Fifth, the Japanese are well-educated; their health system is good; they have the world's highest longevity. Sixth, there is close cooperation between the state, the government bureaucracy, and private banks and industry. Seventh, Japan enjoyed especially favorable market conditions in the post–World War II period, including special access to the U.S. market.

We now think of Japan as among our most reliable Asian allies, but it was not always so. In World War II, it attacked us at Pearl Harbor and was allied with the Axis Powers. There are still tensions in the relationship but now we think of Japan as a close ally and a bulwark of Asia.

The United States would like to have Japan, as a stable and responsible country, play a larger role in world, and especially Asian, affairs. We would like to see Japan as a permanent member of the Security Council at the UN and as a restraint on North Korea's nuclear weapons as well as China's boundless ambitions. But the World War II experience of massive destruction and defeat has left the Japanese wary of international entanglements, and the Japanese Constitution explicitly prohibits the development of nuclear weapons and the sending of Japanese troops abroad. But Japan is slowly overcoming these restrictions in both the Constitution and public opinion and is gradually taking on greater international responsibility.

It is doubtful, however, that Japan will be willing to do in Asia all that the United States would like. Meanwhile, we should remember that Japan has its own long-standing security issues: as a rival (and previous occupier) of China, as both a rival and, in Japan's eyes, a patron of Korea, and as a competitive foe of Russia, particularly in the Kuril Islands, which both countries claim. At the same time, while Japan is not a nuclear power now (because it was bombed by nuclear weapons in World War II), most security analysts believe that, with its hi-tech economy, Japan, if it wished to, could become a nuclear power almost literally overnight.

The "Four Tigers"

The Four Tigers are South Korea, Taiwan, Hong Kong, and Singapore. Following Japan and utilizing essentially the same political-economic development model, all four of these have achieved miracle economic growth and have taken their place among the most prosperous countries in the world.

The Korean Peninsula was once one of the poorest areas of Asia. Divided after World War II between the Communist North (Democratic Peoples' Republic of Korea) and a more Free World–oriented South (Republic of Korea—ROC), it remained a poor, Third World area until the 1970s. South Korea's takeoff began under military-authoritarian rule, but over time the country became a near-classic case of how economic development leads to social change that, in turn in the late 1980s, led to greater pluralism and eventually democracy. Today South Korea is not only a booming First World country but also a *world* leader in such future-oriented indicators as patents, numbers of PhDs, investment, and education—to say nothing of women golfers: twelve of the top twenty players!

Both South Korea and Taiwan have what might be called one-issue foreign policy preoccupations. In South Korea the preoccupation is North Korea and its leader Kim Jong Il and the possibility of their aggression against the ROC. The North has nuclear weapons; the presumption is that the South has them, too, though secret, or could develop them very rapidly. Meanwhile, the South, allied with and protected by the United States, assumes that, like Germany, the Peninsula will one day be reunited under a democratic and capitalistic system. But given Korea's drive, energy, and ambition, that may not be an outcome that its big neighbors—China, Japan, and Russia, too—will want to see.

Taiwan, another Tiger economy, had different origins than South Korea, but its developmental trajectory is almost exactly the same. Taiwan was a Japanese island through World War II; after the communists took control in mainland China in 1948, the remnants of the conservative, or Nationalist, movement fled across the straits to Taiwan. There they established an authoritarian, one-party state not all that different from South Korea. Energetic and hardworking, Taiwan began to achieve miracle growth rates. Its course of development was again parallel to that of South Korea: economic development first, then social change, finally democratization in the late 1980s. Today both South Korea and Taiwan are thriving economic powerhouses and vigorous democracies.

Taiwan has allied itself closely with the United States and is heavily dependent on it. Its great fear and almost exclusive foreign policy preoccupation is that it will be increasingly isolated and eventually overrun by mainland (communist) China, which outnumbers it in population by a ratio of 65:1. Taiwan views the United States as its great protector, although U.S. support has wavered over the years; Japan also provides support. Mainland China assumes that small Taiwan will eventually fall into its hands like ripe fruit, while small Taiwan likes to think it will one day convert gigantic communist China to democracy and capitalism!

Hong Kong was a British colony for a century and a half; in 1998 it became independent from Great Britain but a part of China. It grew as a major banking, commercial, insurance, shipping, and trading center mainly for goods entering or exiting China. Hong Kong itself is only the size of a city-state, consisting of a small enclave on China's mainland and several offshore islands, but it profits enormously as the commercial gateway to big, booming China. It is predominantly a middle-class society and its per capita income makes it one of the richest places in the world.

Since it is now a part of China, Hong Kong has no independent foreign policy. But like Taiwan, its relations with China are its number one and virtually only preoccupation. Though it identifies with Chinese nationalism, accomplishments, and aspirations, Hong Kong's great fear is that one day its giant communist master will clamp down on the city's booming capitalism and spirit of freedom. Hong Kong has a thriving civil society life to prevent that from happening; like Taiwan, it believes it can convert the mainland to democracy and freedom rather than the mainland overwhelming Hong Kong with its communism and authoritarianism. Unlike Taiwan, however, Hong Kong has no international power (the United States) capable of protecting it.

Singapore is another dynamic city-state-size country of five million people but, unlike Hong Kong, it is fully independent and has its own foreign policy. As a former British colony and now a commercial, trading, insurance, and banking center for all of South and Southeast Asia, Singapore has become one of the world's wealthiest, most affluent countries. It has an excellent educational system, excellent health care, and virtually no poverty. It is clean, efficient, and well-run. For a long time under Lee Kwan Yew, the government was top-down and semiauthoritarian; now it is freer and more open—definitely not a police state but not fully liberal either. It has gone from Third World to First World in only forty years.

Singapore's security problems center on its small size and its location. As a small country, Singapore feels it cannot afford to make any mistakes; that is one reason for its tight controls on drugs, crime, and political activity. Located on an island at the tip of the Malay Peninsula, Singapore is surrounded by much larger neighbors— Malaysia, Indonesia, India—who covet its wealth and strategic resources. Hence, Singapore not only runs a tight ship domestically, but it is extremely vigilant regarding drugs, border crossings, and illegal immigrants. The United States could learn a lot from Singapore, which, incidentally, advertises that it will give automatic citizenship to anyone with a PhD!

China

China is, of course, *huge*, in reality as well as metaphorically. It is first in the world in population (1.3 billion), fourth in territory (behind Russia, Canada, and the United States), and second in gross national income (behind only the United States). Its economy is the most dynamic in the world, with growth rates averaging about 10 percent per year over a sustained period, and a huge industrial base and a productive workforce. But, in addition, we all have an image of China as a future world power, even a superpower, perhaps eventually surpassing even the United States. Certainly, the American Department of Defense is gearing up to treat China as our great superpower rival in the twenty-first century.

China is an old society, going back thousands of years, but a relatively new nation. The influence of its culture reaches into such neighboring countries as the two Koreas, Japan, Taiwan, Hong Kong, Macao, Vietnam, and Singapore—several of which (Taiwan, Hong Kong, Macao) could conceivably be fully absorbed into the Chinese nation. In other countries, the Philippines, Indonesia, Malaysia, and Southeast Asia, Chinese minorities are wealthy and powerful, admire China's recent accomplishments, and could conceivably serve as a "Fifth Column" for future Chinese expansionism. China's foreign policy is expansionist, and it is registering major gains in Asia, Africa, the Middle East, and Latin America. In many respects, China seems to be the country of the future.

But I am not so sure. First, China remains a very poor country; with all the attention devoted recently to its growth, we forget that its per capita income is only $5,370, which puts it still at Third World levels and only one-ninth that of the United States. Second, China remains a communist country; I'm not sure it has the flexibility and pragmatism necessary to make the transition to a modern, global power. Third, China is undergoing vast and unprecedented social changes that could well destabilize the country. Think of these numbers: China has 1.3 *billion* people. As industrialization continues, roughly two-thirds of these—approximately *900 million*—will likely migrate from rural to urban areas in the next generation or two. Never in the history of the world has any country undergone that amount of urbanization, with those numbers of people, in such a short period of time. Think of the impact of those numbers on jobs, water supplies, electricity, pollution, sewage, housing, infrastructure, health care, and the environment.

Can China survive these immense pressures? Can it hold together under the impact of such vast changes? Many China observers and students of development do not think so. For the road to national development and societal modernization is full of pitfalls and often revolution, civil wars, and the potential for national breakdowns. China is not immune to these possibilities. In addition, in China, almost no one believes the official ideology of Marxism-Leninism anymore; the central government is losing its control over some cities and regions; social change is accelerating and may be getting out-of-hand; the people are demanding greater freedom and liberty; and the bureaucracy is massively inefficient and corrupt. The odds of China reaching superpower status or, alternatively, breaking down into chaos and fragmentation are about fifty-fifty.

China wants to be treated as a great power, even a global superpower. To that end, it is expanding and modernizing its army, navy, air force, and space programs. It is reaching out and building diplomatic and commercial relations in Africa and Latin America. It projects its power throughout the Indian Ocean, the South China Sea, and the western Pacific. It is cooperating with Russia through treaty arrangements and along its long northern border. But at the same time it is hemmed in by Japan, Korea, Russia, and India, and by U.S. security agreements with these same countries, which look very similar to the old Containment strategy used in the Cold War against the Soviet Union.

China's future remains unknown. On the one hand, it is a tremendously dynamic, energetic, productive country that is growing rapidly. On the other, it faces tremendous internal obstacles and divisions; and internationally its expansionist ambitions seem to be checked for now. So those odds cited earlier about China's possibilities seem about right: fifty-fifty.

India

India is another potential big player in international affairs. It is the world's second largest nation in population (1.1 billion) and has ambitious to surpass China as the largest country by about 2040. It is the seventh largest nation in size but only one-third the size of the United States: imagine 1.1 billion people in a territory equal to the United States east of the Mississippi. It is twelfth worldwide in gross national income, but on a per capita basis it is down there with Nicaragua at Third World levels, and only half the level of China. At the same time and in contrast to China, India is the world's largest democracy.

India is another country with a very long history as a culture and society but a short history (since 1947) as a nation-state. It is a predominantly Hindu society but also 20 percent Muslim; in fact, India is one of the most complex societies in the world, divided not only according to religion but also by ethnic, racial, class, caste, and regional variation. It would require a *lifetime* of study to understand India in all its complexity.

For a long time, India's democracy was celebrated, but its economic growth record was anemic, far behind China, Brazil, and other more dynamic Third World countries. Then India made a breakthrough, abandoned its earlier efforts at socialism and statism, and allowed the free marketplace to rule. The result: India soared—not quite at the level of China but no longer so far behind. At the same time, India remains a very poor, Third World country. Think of it this way: even if only one-fifth of the Indian population

(246 million people) have made it to middle-class ranks, that is still a consumer market almost equal to the United States. The same criteria applied to China yields a middle-class consumer market of 263 million; no wonder U.S. (and other) companies are eager to tap these markets.

India's size, population, and growing economic might make it a force to be reckoned with in international affairs, especially regionally but now, like China, increasingly globally as well. India projects its power into the Indian Ocean and toward its closest neighbors on the South Asian subcontinent. It is very worried about China and its expansion into Tibet and other areas on India's high (Himalayan) northern frontier. But its main preoccupation is rival (and Muslim) Pakistan, only one-fourth the size of India and with one-sixth its population. India and Pakistan, both nuclear powers, have fought four (nonnuclear) wars since they both became independent after World War II; they also conduct irregular warfare over the province of Kashmir, which is under Indian control but has a majority-Muslim population. Meanwhile, the United States seeks an alliance with Pakistan in its war against the Taliban in Afghanistan, while also signing a broad-ranging nuclear treaty with India, and India allies with Russia as a check on China's expansionist tendencies.

India is an emerging power, an impressive if sometimes chaotic democracy, and a country that is getting its act together to achieve sustained economic growth. It is one of the large, emerging countries that is a candidate for the UN Security Council. Along with China, Japan, and Russia, it is one of the big and important Asian powers.

Indonesia

Indonesia is the world's fourth most-populous nation (226 million, behind only China, India, and the United States), and for that reason has long been considered—along with China, India, Egypt, Nigeria, South Africa, Brazil, and Mexico—as one of the key nations in the developing world.

Indonesia consists of thirteen thousand islands in a long archipelago that is as wide as the United States from New York to San Francisco.

The archipelago looks like an extension of the Malay Peninsula, and indeed the ethnic identity of most Indonesians probably derives from Malaysia as well as indigenously. Indonesia is the world's largest majority-Muslim nation, though its practices of Islam have generally been more easygoing and mixed with indigenous beliefs than Islam elsewhere. But the island of Bali is majority-Hindu, and in other islands of the archipelago there are Buddhist and Christian, both Catholic and Protestant communities—sometimes at each others' throats. The islands also differ greatly in their level of development, with Java and Sumatra the most developed and some others almost completely isolated from modern civilization. The national average income of $3,980 per person per year puts Indonesia in the Third World category, above India but considerably behind China.

For three hundred years, Indonesia was a Dutch slave-plantation economy, through World War II. Unfortunately, the Dutch never equipped the colony for self-government, and when independence came in the late 1940s–early 1950s, Indonesia was ill-prepared for it. It had no government, no bureaucracy, no educational system, no armed forces, and no infrastructure. Unsurprisingly, its first years of independence were disorganized and chaotic; when the Army under General Suharto took over in 1966, order was restored and the economy began to grow even while human rights were widely abused. In 1998 democracy was restored and Indonesia has been operating since then as a democratic but wobbly state.

Indonesia's main preoccupation is not so much international as domestic: how to hold this very disparate island chain together, how to knit together as a nation many different peoples and ethnicities, and how to achieve sustained national development. Its most pressing international issues are often within its own territories or along its sometimes obscure island borders: with the former Portuguese territory of East Timor, with Malaysia, and with Papua New Guinea. It also has disputes mainly over drug trafficking, immigration, and now terrorism with Australia and Singapore. Meanwhile, recognizing its size and strategic importance straddling all the sea lanes between the Indian and Pacific Oceans and as a possible base for international terrorism, the United States has sought to maintain good relations with Indonesia and aid its development.

The Philippines

The Philippines is another Southeast Asian island nation like Indonesia. Its population of eighty-eight million is diverse, spread over thousands of islands, and, again like Indonesia, derived ethnically from a mix of indigenous, Malay, and by this time more diverse elements. Its per capita income is $3,730 per year, Third World level, but that disguises great disparities: very poor in the southern islands where there is still a vicious guerrilla struggle underway, and better off in the northern island of Luzon where the capital, Manila, is located. The Philippines, like Indonesia, supports the so-called chopstick theory of development: no Chinese or Chinese culture, so no or weak development!

The Philippines was a Spanish colony for four hundred years and a U.S. colony for one hundred. Interesting parallels are provided by Puerto Rico, Panama, and Cuba. The Philippines was and is a "Latin"-Catholic country in the middle of a mainly Malay sea; it also adopted baseball and the English language from the Americans. The United States established military bases in the Philippines and, even after independence in 1934, closely oversaw Philippine politics. Like Indonesia, the country was governed democratically, if unstably, during its early independence history, then succumbed to the dictatorship (1965–1986, supported by the United States) of Ferdinand Marcos, and since 1986 has restored a still-shaky democracy. Though having lost most of its bases in the islands some years before, the United States still watches semi-paternally over Philippine affairs.

The Philippines' main policy issues are domestic, not international—again a familiar theme. Those include: holding a very diverse society together, preventing the nation from disintegrating, defeating the insurgency, and achieving development. International issues, in this island nation where the sea provides a defensive perimeter, are generally of a secondary nature, having to do mainly with immigration and emigration, defending the rights of Filipinos working abroad, and now international terrorism. The United States, as with Indonesia, wants to maintain a stable, democratic Philippines and has been supportive of its developmental and counterterrorism efforts.

The Newest Tigers

Japan was the first "Asian Tiger," followed by South Korea, Taiwan, Hong Kong, and Singapore. All five of these have now made break-throughs to join the world of the developed nations. But those break-throughs came thirty and more years ago; now the original "Tigers" have been joined by other nations following essentially the same model of state-led capitalism. The latest "Tigers" include China, of course, but also Malaysia, Thailand, and Vietnam. It is too early to call either Indonesia or the Philippines a "Tiger," but their economies are growing, too, though more slowly.

The most developed part of Malaysia, and the capital of Kuala Lumpur, lies just north of Singapore on the Malay Peninsula. But it also includes numerous small islands as well as about one-third of the island of Borneo. Malaysia's per capita income of $13,570 places it way behind the other "Tigers" but way ahead of China, India, Indonesia, and the Philippines. Long torn by internal political and ethnic con-flict, Malaysia got its act together and began to prosper under outspo-ken Prime Minister Mahathir bin Mohamad. It is a Muslim-majority country but generally a tolerant one; the fact that it is Islamic has not prevented it from modernization and growth. Malaysia's main security problems stem from its location on a narrow peninsula, its proximity to much poorer Indonesia, and its command of the crucial (and pirate-filled) Straits of Malacca. Drugs, terrorism, and illegal immigration are main issues.

Just north of Malaysia on the Malay Peninsula and then extend-ing into Indochina is the country of Thailand. Long a peaceful if sleepy country, Thailand was caught up in the Vietnam War but was not heavily bombed as the other countries of the area (Cambodia, Laos, Vietnam) were. So Thailand recovered quickly after the war. It is a major agricultural producer, now has manufacturing as well, and its beaches are a haven for tourists. With a new and efficient international airport and a central (for the region) location, its capi-tal of Bangkok has become a hub of banking, finance, and business, not yet rivaling Hong Kong, Singapore, or even Kuala Lumpur but booming nonetheless. Thailand's per capita income has climbed to $7,800, still ahead of China but behind its wealthier neighbors. Its foreign policy problems stem mainly from local rivalries and because it is surrounded by poor countries: Cambodia, Laos, and Myanmar. Drugs, crime, terrorism, and illegal immigration are main issues.

Vietnam, a former French colony, was long divided between a communist North and the noncommunist South. After a long civil war, which also included a North Vietnam invasion of the South and the defeat of U.S. forces brought in to help the South, Vietnam was finally united in the 1970s under communist and North Vietnamese authority. That fact plus the devastation of the war years slowed Vietnam's development. But following the Chinese model of a strong Leninist state, Vietnam began to recover in the 1990s and today is becoming a major exporter. Its per capita income at $2,550 is still low, at India levels, but Vietnam is energetic and disciplined, and few doubt its takeoff will continue. Vietnam strives to ward off its large neighbor China while also worrying about its long western border with even poorer Cambodia and Laos.

Australia and New Zealand

Australia and New Zealand are anomalies: two white, European outposts, with essentially European cultures and living standards ($33,340 per capita in Australia, $26,340 in New Zealand), "stuck" out here in the middle of Asia and surrounded by Asian nations. Come to think of it, that's not all that different, is it, from Canada, the United States, or South Africa: similar European enclaves stuck out in the middle of non-European continents?

The islands that make up Australia and New Zealand were discovered by the Spanish, Portuguese, and Dutch back in the sixteenth century, but they were largely ignored and left unsettled in favor of more valuable colonies found elsewhere. Only in the early nineteenth century, and then under British control, did the islands begin to be populated and to develop as the fragments of European civilization that we know them as today.

By culture, history, family background, and preference, Australia and New Zealand were far more oriented toward Europe than Asia. Racism was also long present in their attitudes toward Asia as well as toward the indigenous peoples who had long lived on the islands. Meanwhile, the rest of Asia resented Australia and New Zealand for their condescending attitudes and eyed the vast, empty spaces of interior Australia as compared to their crowded conditions.

A number of these conditions are now changing. After all these generations, Australia and New Zealand are less oriented toward Europe; they have begun to think of themselves as "Asian" nations. They are more integrated into Asian trade and security arrangements; the islanders more often take their vacations in Asia; there is less racism and more intermingling. Australia and New Zealand, not altogether unlike Western Europe or the United States, have also somewhat relaxed (but not abolished) their immigration policies to admit more Asians.

Both Australia and New Zealand have very tough, well-trained security forces to deal with any local or regional disturbances. Drugs, terrorism, and illegal immigration are the main issues. Because they speak English and come mainly from the same European background, these security forces are closely integrated into U.S. defense planning and are frequently used either on their own or as backup to U.S. forces. If you ask Americans what countries they feel warmest toward ("thermometer readings"), fellow English-speakers Australia, Canada, Great Britain, and New Zealand top the list every time.

Non-Tigers

After all this discussion of the "Asian miracle" and the "Asian century," it may seem surprising to some that there are still countries in Asia that are not doing well, that have not yet begun their economic takeoff. These include Vietnam's neighbors Cambodia and Laos, Thailand's neighbor Myanmar, India's Eastern neighbor Bangladesh, North Korea, and the former Portuguese colony that is part of the Indonesia archipelago, East Timor.

All of these countries have per capita incomes below $2,000 per year. That puts them not only at Third World levels but at the lowest of Third World levels, with poverty, malnutrition, and disease comparable to the worst cases in Africa and Latin America. These are very poor countries, still largely outside the mainstream of global commerce and business, and not much yet involved in international politics—except as their very poverty causes breakdowns, failed states, and chaos, and thereby occasioning outside intervention, as in the case of East Timor. But even in these countries the Asian success story begins to have an impact; even among the poorest of the poor, the earliest glimmerings of economic growth are beginning to take place.

A special case is that of North Korea. Here we have one of the world's poorest nations, headed by an uncertain (some would say "crazy") leadership, that happens to have nuclear weapons and the means to deliver them. North Korea's leaders want respect, security, and some assurance that outside powers (China, Japan, United States) will not attack them; meanwhile, North Korea's neighbors and the United States, not trusting the leadership, have been pressuring the North to stop its weapons development. That may happen in the short run; meanwhile, long term, there may be hope for the reunification of the peninsula, but that would be, given the large disparities, an even more difficult and expensive process than the unification of East and West Germany.

Conclusion

Power in international affairs keeps on shifting. It is now, undoubtedly, shifting to Asia. Bank robbers, when asked why they rob banks, proverbially reply, "Because that's where the money is"; one could say much the same thing about Asia's place in international affairs. Because so much money, industry, banking, manufacturing, and so on have over the last forty years shifted to Asia, that's also where our foreign policy concentration has shifted. Asia has now replaced Europe as the main focus of our foreign policy. Asia's incredible economic development in the last half century also makes Latin America, the Middle East, and Africa look bad by comparison. Today, Asia is where the main action is.

Asia has seven or eight of the world's most dynamic economies. China is number two in the world in terms of gross national income, Japan, number three. South Korea, Taiwan, Hong Kong, and Singapore are tremendously dynamic societies, booming ahead. And now Malaysia, Thailand, Vietnam, and perhaps others are poised to join the earlier "Tigers." China holds so much U.S. debt paper that if it decides it wants to cash in, the entire U.S. economy would be near collapse. South Korea is in the top five worldwide on so many indices (patents, education, investment, etc.) that it could in the future well become a major global player.

Five of the Asian countries (Russia, North Korea, China, India, and Pakistan) have nuclear weapons; at least three others (South Korea, Taiwan, and Japan) may have them secretly or have the technology to develop them almost literally overnight. Moreover, many of these countries have long-standing border disputes and other disagreements with their neighbors: Russia-China, Russia-Japan, China-Japan, North Korea-South Korea, China-Taiwan, China-India, and India-Pakistan. And those are only the major, especially volatile disputes; numerous smaller rivalries and potential conflicts also exist. So in Asia we are witnessing not only unprecedented economic growth but also, at the same time, the serious potential for conflict and even war.

And yet, despite the possibilities for conflict, Asia lacks the institutional mechanisms for resolving such potential conflicts. Unlike Europe, which has both NATO and the EU, Asia does not have a network of pan-Asian organizations, such as ASEAN, capable of resolving conflicts and keeping the peace. Such organizations are forming but slowly, and they lack the enforcement mechanisms that Europe has. In the absence of a region-wide security apparatus, the United States pursues a balance-of-power strategy in Asia: India and Pakistan balancing each other off, North Korea and South Korea, India counterbalancing China, Japan and South Korea also balancing China, China and Russia checking each other. In the absence of consensus or strong institutions to resolve conflicts among these powerful and ambitious rivals, a balance-of-power strategy seems to be the best policy to pursue. The United States is active and a partner is all these balance of power strategies.

That is one of the reasons the United States is so heavily involved in Asia. In addition to Asia's economic importance to us, we are looked on as a global peacemaker by the Asian nations, the only honest broker, and a useful interlocutor in all those disputes mentioned earlier. That is also why, in the absence of very many Asian multilateral institutions, we have major bilateral treaties with so many countries of the area: Japan, South Korea, China, India, Pakistan, the Philippines, Indonesia, and others. All of these are BIG-TIME treaties, with major powers, involving high stakes and major U.S. economic and strategic interests, now and in the future. Those are among the reasons that Asia is emerging—has already emerged—as the most important area in the world for the United States, and why it is likely to remain so far into the future.

Note

1. In some places, this is jokingly known as the "chopstick theory" of development. Thus, Japan, China, South Korea, Taiwan, Hong Kong, Macao, Singapore, and Vietnam (all chopstick users) are forging ahead, while Indonesia and the Philippines (non-chopstick users) lag behind.

Suggested Readings

Curtis, Gerald. *The Logic of Japanese Politics* (New York: Columbia University Press, 1999).

DeBary, William T. *Asian Values and Human Rights* (Cambridge, MA: Harvard University Press, 1998).

He, Baogang. *The Democratic Implications of Civil Society in China* (New York: St Martin's, 1997).

Jenson, Lionel. *Manufacturing Confucianism: Chinese Traditions and Universal Civilization* (Durham, NC: Duke University Press, 1997).

Lee, Juan Yew. *From Third World to First: The Singapore Story* (Singapore: Marshall Cavendish Eds., 2010).

Lie, John. *Han Unbound: The Political Economy of South Korea* (Stanford, CA: Stanford University Press, 1998).

Moody, Peter. *Political Opposition in Post-Confucian Society* (New York: Praeger, 1988).

Nathan, Andrew. *Chinese Democracy* (New York: Knopf, 1985).

Pye, Lucian. *Asian Power and Politics: The Cultural Dimension of Authority* (Cambridge, MA: Belknap Press, 1985).

Robinson, Thomas (ed.). *Democracy and Development in East Asia* (Washington, D.C.: American Enterprise Institute, 1991).

CHAPTER 6

The Middle East

The area known as "the Middle East" (so named because it was halfway to Asia—"the Far East") is, from the point of view of U.S. foreign policy, the most troublesome region in the world. Think of the main strategic interests that we have there: oil, without which the economies of the developed countries (Japan as well as Europe and the United States) would go right down the drain, terrorism, and Israel, the only democracy and the United States' only ally in the region.

Then think of all the conflicts going on there that have the potential to threaten those vital interests: the war in Iraq, the war in Afghanistan, the nuclear standoff with Iran, the war against terrorism, the war against Al Qaeda, the Israeli-Palestine conflict, the possible destabilization of nuclear Pakistan, revolutionary movements aimed at toppling Saudi Arabia, Kuwait, Bahrain, and the United Arab Emirates (UAE), terrorist groups in Lebanon and Gaza, instability in Central Asia—all the main U.S. allies and oil suppliers. And more revolutionary movements aimed at toppling the governments in Egypt, Morocco, Syria, Lebanon—all friends or allies of the United States, plus the subversion of Hezbollah in Lebanon and Hamas in Palestine. Add to all this the widespread Muslim hatred in the Middle East toward the West and the United States in particular, and you have a truly dangerous situation.

Adding to our difficulties is the fact the Middle East seems to be impervious to reform, or at least the kind of reform the United States seeks to promote. Of all the regions of the world, the Middle East is the least democratic, with only Turkey and Israel (and *none* of the Arab countries) classified as democracies. Similarly with economics: it is oil, not economic reform, industriousness, or hard work, that has been almost solely responsible for the newfound wealth of Bahrain, Kuwait, Saudi Arabia, Qatar, Oman, the UAE, Iran, and Libya, the most prosperous of the Middle Eastern countries. Most of us like to think it is hard work and merit that pay off for countries in development, but in the Middle East it is the sheer luck—like winning the lottery—of sitting atop vast oil deposits that accounts for the difference between rich and poor states. In addition, *nowhere* in the Middle East have we seen the kind of sequences that we've seen so strongly in Asia and Latin America: economic development and industrialization lead to social change and pluralism, and pluralism socially leads to pluralism politically and, hence, to democratization. In the Middle East, none of these processes that figure so prominently in the comparative politics and developing areas literature has worked as they have in other areas.

A number of reasons have been suggested as to why the Middle East lags behind, why its development is so disappointing. The first reason is geography and climate: hot, infertile, desert conditions in much of the area. A second reason is foreign interference and colonialism, which drained its resources and skewed its path to development. A third reason is weak or absent institutions: weak parliaments, weak judiciaries, weak bureaucracies, and weak civil society. Fourth, there is the prevailing political system: regimes in power (Saleh, Assad, the Iranian Mullahs, the Saudis, King Hussein, Qaddafi, Saddam Hussein until the United States overthrew him) are powerful and oppressive while the opposition (democratic, socialist, fundamentalist) tends to be weak, divided, and unable to get to power.

All these reasons for the Middle East's lack of development are important, but the most important one may well be cultural or, more accurately, political-cultural. The issue is that both the Koran and Islamic sharia laws provide abundant justification for authoritarianism and top-down, male rule, but they are very weak on such topics as human rights, pluralism, citizen participation, and democracy. In addition, the Koran and sharia law condemn "usury," including the earning or charging of interest, which makes it very difficult to have banks, lending agencies, or financial institutions. Currently, some of these difficulties are being overcome through so-called Islamic banks, but the barriers are still so large that foreign as well as domestic investors may prefer to put their money elsewhere. We cannot say that this Islamic political culture is determinative in holding back democracy and development, but it has certainly put powerful obstacles in the way. It is striking that *none* of the Arab Middle Eastern countries is a democracy or has made it to First World economic rank.

And yet, change and some limited development continue to go forward in the Arab world. Oil has been the main agent triggering development; without oil in the Middle East, you are usually condemned to continued poverty. In the oil-rich countries there is now more wealth than before; the middle class is growing larger; and those at the bottom of the social scale are rising. The governments of these countries are being obliged to provide more social services (health, education, housing, social welfare) and that in turn produces even more changes. Pluralism, civil society, and opposition movements are growing but are not yet sufficiently strong to supplant the governments in power. All this means that while there have been *no* democratic breakthroughs, the Middle Eastern countries are not stagnant either, and change is in the air. Popular movements are growing.

Socioeconomic Analysis

The Middle East has among the most skewed income levels in the world (see table 6.1). It has very rich countries (Kuwait, Bahrain, Israel, Saudi Arabia) and very poor ones too (Djibouti, Yemen). And many countries, not quite so poor, but not wealthy either, that the World Bank calls "lower middle income"—for example, Morocco, Egypt, Jordan, Syria. What it lacks are stable, progressing, developing countries in between the extremes that have good, solid prospects for the future. Turkey may be the only country that falls safely in this last category of stable, democratic, *upper*-middle-income countries.

In addition to the extremes between countries, income *within* these countries is terribly unevenly distributed. The gaps between rich and poor tend to be very wide. There is very little middle class on which a stable democracy can be built.

Table 6.1 Per capita income in the Middle East

Country	Per capita income (in $)	Category
Afghanistan	–	LIC
Algeria	7,640	LMC
Armenia	5,900	LMC
Azerbaijan	6,370	LMC
Bahrain	34,310	HI
Djibouti	2,260	LMC
Egypt	5,400	LMC
Iran	10,800	LMC
Iraq	–	LMC
Israel	25,930	HI
Jordan	5,100	LMC
Kazakhstan	9,700	UMC
Kuwait	49,970	HI
Kurgyz Republic	1,950	LIC
Lebanon	10,050	UMC
Libya	14,710	UMC
Morocco	3,990	LMC
Oman	19,740	HI
Qatar		HI
Saudi Arabia	22,910	HI
Syria	4,370	LMC
Tajikistan	1,710	LIC
Tunisia	7,130	LMC
Turkey	12,090	UMC
Turkmenistan	4,350	LMC
United Arab Emirates		HI
Uzbekistan	2,430	LIC
West Bank and Gaza		LMC
Yemen	2,200	LIC

HI: High-income country; UMC: Upper middle income country; LMC: Lower middle income country; LIC: Low-income country.

But the situation in the Middle East is more complicated than that. If it were just a matter of large income gaps between the rich and the poor, we could say that the Middle East is just like Latin America in this regard, or perhaps like the Philippines, Indonesia, and other developing areas. But it is not. First, in the oil-rich Middle Eastern countries (Kuwait, Bahrain, Saudi Arabia, Qatar, the United Arab Emirates), at least within the ruling family and among citizens, everyone is pretty well off. Oil is, in this sense, a blessing; on balance, it's better to be rich in oil than poor—like Yemen. On the other hand, oil can be a double-edged sword, the logic being this: if we are so rich (in oil), why should we work at all? Oil brings higher living standards, but it also brings complacency, laziness, a reliance on government largesse, and an attitude of "why work"?

In addition, because these countries are so rich and their citizens often averse to physical labor, they must import laborers from other countries. These include workers from Indonesia, the Sudan, the Philippines, India, Bangladesh, Palestine, and other countries. Often the conditions for these laborers, who are usually there for years without their families, are abysmal. They live in Spartan quarters and, while the pay is good, are treated shabbily by the host government. They are not allowed to mingle with the host country population, nor is there a path to citizenship for them. You can be sure that the host government's intelligence services also keep a close eye on them to prevent strikes, violence, and terrorist incidents. Hence, while the oil-rich states do not have a working-class proletariat of their own, they do have an imported one, in the form of all those imported workers of whom they maintain tight surveillance. But they also worry a great deal that all these imported workers might form a revolutionary, a destabilizing, or a terrorist threat within their own societies.

Social mobility works the same way. For the oil-rich Saudis, Kuwaitis, Bahranians, Qatarians, and residents of the UAE, there is so much money around that one can rise in the social scale. Even Bedouins can rise in this way. But social mobility is *only* for Saudis, Kuwaitis, and so on. If you are a foreigner or one of those imported laborers mentioned earlier, there is no upward mobility for you. You are *completely outside* the indigenous social system. You don't fit! And, in the absence of any possibility of citizenship, there is no possibility for you to integrate into the local society or to improve your lot. You are a nonperson in the local society's terms.

But if you are a Saudi, a Kuwaiti, and so on, life for you can be very comfortable. *Everything* is paid for: education, health care, other amenities. The government does this purposely as a way of heading off revolt or revolution. For here is the dilemma: the oil-rich states of the Persian Gulf are still basically feudal monarchies: old-fashioned, very traditional, anachronistic, one would think doomed in the modern world. How can they possibly last? The answer is: by sharing the wealth, by providing elaborate social programs, by giving their peoples all they want. Here is one of the places in the world where the wealth has actually trickled down. And consciously so, as part of a concerted government and royal family plan to head off any possible revolutionary, or even democratic, movement by co-opting or buying off any possible middle- or lower-class discontent even before it happens.

Interestingly, the less-rich states of the Middle East have employed a very similar strategy. These are not the poorest or LIC states (they have no money) but the lower-middle-income (LMC) and upper-middle-income (UMC) countries whose economies have been growing, though modestly, in recent years. Here we are talking of Algeria, Egypt, Jordan, Lebanon, Libya, Morocco, Syria, and Tunisia. In *all* of these, the regime in power, as a way of heading off Islamic fundamentalism or possible revolution from below, has been funneling money down into the lower levels of the social system. The programs include higher wages, better health care, education, better social programs, and a general raising of living standards. The strategy behind this effort is mainly political: to keep the regime that dispenses these programs in power, to benefit the emerging and middle classes, and to prevent opposition elements from establishing a strong base from which to topple the regime.

Countries like Yemen (North and South) and Djibouti cannot practice this strategy. They lack the funds for almost any kind of social program. Not only are they the poorest countries in the region but—and there is a correlation here—they are also the most unstable; their governments, most prone to being overthrown; they are the most likely to become failed states; and they are also most likely to become havens for terrorist activities. Here again we see a close relationship between international relations and comparative politics: those countries that are the least successful at development are likely to become the most problematic for U.S. foreign policy.

Israel is, of course, an exception to all these rules. It is a country *geographically* located in the Middle East. It is not Arab or Muslim, but a majority Jewish state with a large Palestinian minority. In cultural, social, and political terms, it is Western and European more than it is Middle Eastern, though that is gradually changing. It has a high per capita income (comparable to the poorer countries of Europe, Greece, Spain, or Portugal) but not as high as Kuwait or Bahrain—though higher than Saudi Arabia. It is the *only* country in the Middle East that is democratic and the only one that is both democratic and developed.

Which gets us to the last set of questions: why have the other countries of the Middle East been so unsuccessful with both development and democracy? What is holding them back? Why have they not achieved like the Asian countries have achieved—indeed, at "miracle" growth rates? Why are they mired at roughly the same developmental levels as Latin America—but generally above the level of most of Africa? And why *no* democracies at all? What's wrong with the Middle East, with the Arab countries, with the Muslim states? I'm including in these questions the rich states of Bahrain, Saudi Arabia, Kuwait, and the UAE because, while they're rich, they're certainly not democratic. And because I believe it's not altogether fair if a country gets rich on the basis of oil alone without any other redeeming virtues, such as merit, hard work, and achievement.

The answers to these questions are complex. There is no one easy or simple answer. Part of the answer lies in the fact of colonial control—chiefly France and Great Britain—over this area for a long time and the failure of the colonial powers to develop local government, bureaucracies, educational systems, and armies. Part of the answer also lies in the absence of very many resources, other than oil, in the region: you can't very well create more wealth if you have little wealth to begin with. Part of it lies in the rigid, hierarchical social structure of the area and the fact they are, for the most part, still tribal and ethnically divided societies rather than unified national ones.

A key explanation for both the lack of democracy and the lack of development in the region has to do with the structure of power in these countries. The facts are that most of these are strong, authoritarian, and top-down regimes (not just the Gulf monarchies but also Saleh in Yemen, Qaddafi in Libya, Abdullah in Jordan, Assad in Syria), while their oppositions are weak. Civil societies are either oppressed by the regimes in power or they are controlled by corporatist control mechanisms that turn them into government-run trade unions, political parties, and interest groups. There is little social or political pluralism here, few checks and balances, and only a weak and not independent press. And if these strong states can control their secular opposition, the fundamentalists in their ranks, meanwhile channeling social benefits to the masses, they can stay in power for a long time. Meanwhile popular discontent is rising.

Finally, there is culture. Both the Koran and the sharia law tend to justify strong, authoritarian rule. Neither is supportive of democracy and pluralism. True, they emphasize consultation (with tribal chiefs) and the building of unity and consensus, but that is a long way from democracy. Nor have the recent experiments with strengthening parliaments in Jordan and Kuwait or the holding of elections in Algeria, Iraq, and Afghanistan (under U.S. direction) done much to strengthen democracy. Of all the Islamic countries of the Middle East, only Turkey is a democracy, and even that is subject to several qualifications. I am convinced that it is not just structure and institutions that hold the Middle East back but religion and culture as well.

Background and Context

The Middle East, like China and India, is the home of some very ancient cultures and civilizations, but relatively new nation-states. The Middle East was the founding center of the three main Abrahamic, monotheistic religions: Judaism, Christianity, and Islam; the *Torah*, the *Bible*, and the *Koran*, as well as modern archeology tell the story of these early peoples. From as far back as history records, the Middle East was an area of conflict and competing civilizations: Mesopotamia (present-day Iraq), Persia (present-day Iran), Arabia, Egypt, Jews, Byzantium (present-day Turkey).

In ancient times, both Greece and Rome conquered and had a profound impact on large parts of the area. Greece and Rome brought their cultures as well as their conquering armies; the Middle East absorbed some elements of these Western cultures, while resisting others. From the first to the sixth century AD, Christianity also emanating from the West had a major impact; in later centuries, and continuing to today, the Christian communities would be persecuted and all but exterminated from the Middle East.

In the seventh century AD came Muhammed and the rise of Islam. In those days Islam was a particularly militant as well as militaristic religion; the question on everyone's mind, with large implications for policy, is whether that is still true today. That is, is Islam always an aggressive belief system or can it coexist peacefully with other religions and cultures?

Islam lays claim to being a universal religion and a universal polity, fixed and immutable. It is a community of believers backed by state power; there is no separation of church and state in Islam as there is in the United States. As it emerged in the seventh and eighth centuries, Islam moved from being a state to a far-ranging empire. Islam's conquests in a relatively short period of time were truly phenomenal: throughout the Arabian Peninsula, eastward into India (and eventually down the Malay Peninsula and throughout Indonesia), southward into Africa to include the Nile kingdoms of Egypt and the Sudan, westward across North Africa (Tunisia, Libya, Algeria, Morocco) and all the way to the Atlantic and then across the Straits of Gibraltar into Spain and Portugal, and northwest into Asia Minor (Turkey) and the Balkan countries of southeast Europe, including for different periods of time Bulgaria, Romania, Albania, Kosovo, Bosnia, Hungary, and even southern Austria. Eventually, Islam was halted and turned back to its present-day borders as a result of defeats in Spain (the fifteenth century) and Austria (the seventeenth century).

After overrunning these other huge territories in what in Western Europe we think of as the Middle Ages, the Islamic lands were themselves conquered by invaders from the east. These included the Mongols and Genghis Khan in the twelfth century and, slightly later, the Turks who came originally from the steppes of Asian Russia. Some of these marauding Turkish tribes went directly to Asia Minor (hence, Turkey); others swept south into the Arab lands. What is striking about these conquests is that instead of the conquerors imposing their religion and culture upon the conquered, the conquerors themselves "completely surrendered" (Middle East historian Bernard Lewis's words) to the religion of the conquered: Islam. Then, as the ethnic Mongols and Turks eventually retreated back toward their home territories, they carried with them and implanted in present-day Turkey, southern Russia, and Central Asia the Islamic religion to which they had been exposed in their Middle Eastern conquests. That helps explain why Azerbaijan, the Caucasus, Central Asia, and large areas of southern Russia are Muslim, and why we are justified in including Central Asia in this chapter on the Middle East.

After the Mongol and Turkish conquests had run their course, the Middle East continued to be pulled, and sometimes conquered, from three main directions: Persia in the east, Egypt in the south, and Turkey to the northwest. After the crusades, which only reconquered for Christianity and the West a narrow strip of land along the eastern Mediterranean (present-day Lebanon, Israel, and Gaza), the Islamic world continued to define itself in terms of its conflict with the West. This struggle would go on for a thousand years and more, beginning with expansionist Islamic clash with Christian, Orthodox Byzantium, and arguably continuing to today's "clash of civilizations" (Samuel P. Huntington's term). Meanwhile, in these centuries leading to what we in the West call the modern world, the Islamic world was beset by *internal* conflicts and less by external wars.

During much of this period, which seems hard to believe today, the Islamic world was the leader in science, mathematics, philosophy, and art, and not the West. While the West was still stuck in the "Dark Ages," the Islamic world built great cities, founded great centers of learning, and was generally more sophisticated and cultured than the West. But from the sixteenth century on, these trends were reversed, with the West forging ahead in terms of development and modernization, and the Islamic world came to lag behind. We in the West consider this in our histories a "natural" progression, but in the Middle East the reasons for the area's decline are a subject of immense consternation and self-examination.

The culmination of these criss-crossing trend lines (the Islamic world's decline and the West's increasing ascendance) resulted in a century and a half of Western imperialism in the Middle East from the early nineteenth to the mid-twentieth century. The two chief imperial powers in this part of the world were France and Great Britain, the former going into Egypt and present-day Lebanon and Syria, and the latter into Afghanistan, Pakistan, India, Jordan, and present-day Palestine. These conquests were aided by the economic weakness of the Middle East, the continued existence of tribal politics and lack of a central state, and the long-term decline of the Ottoman (Turkish) Empire.

Meanwhile, two other events or trends were underway that would profoundly impact the Middle East: (1) the discovery of oil, which was used to fuel Europe's industrialization, and (2) the gradual, uneven beginning of modernization in the Middle East under the impact initially of the French Revolution (liberty, equality, fraternity) and other ideas and technologies brought from the outside, as well as increasing self-examination on the part of the Arabs: who are we as a people and a civilization and why are we so far behind the West?

As imperialism began to give way in the twentieth century, the result was the division of the Middle East into the nation-states that we know today. However, the borders left behind by the imperialists, rather like the situation in Africa after imperialism, bore little resemblance whatsoever to the geographic, cultural, ethnic, and tribal realities of the area. They are, like the African countries, artificial states with artificial borders. That goes a long ways toward explaining the continued ethnic and religious strife *within* these countries, the weaknesses of the state and central institutions (organized on ethnic rather than national lines), and the difficulty of following a national policy of development and modernization.

Independence in the Middle East came not all at once but in three waves. First, at the end of World War I, Turkey, Iran, and Afghanistan were fully sovereign states. In the interwar period, second, 1919–1939, Saudi Arabia, Yemen, Iraq, and Egypt achieved independence. Finally, after World War II, Syria, Lebanon, Jordan, and Israel emerged as independent states. Certain other peoples—Kurds, Palestinians, other minority tribal and ethnic groups—founded communities, but not states, a source of continuing friction and problems.

The "new states" of the Middle East faced many of the same problems common to all new states: settling border disputes, establishing a national identity, creating such national institutions as bureaucracies and armies. But they were also torn by internal divisions and often revolts, by conflicts across borders, and by repeated wars, chiefly involving Israel and its Arab neighbors. Repeated interference by the former colonial powers, Britain and France, and now by the Cold War antagonists, the United States and the Soviet Union, added to the region's instability.

With the end of French and British colonialism after World War II, the United States became the major outside actor in the region.

We became both the policeman settling disputes, as between Israel and Arabs for existence, and the fireman putting out brush fires when they occurred. The United States by this time was heavily involved in the Middle East politically, economically, diplomatically, militarily, and through our private oil companies—this was the period when we became heavily dependent on Middle East oil.

The other former powers had been largely exhausted by World War II, but by the 1960s and 1970s the Soviet Union was again heavily involved in the area, particularly in Egypt, Syria, Afghanistan, and Iraq where the Soviets had invested heavily and built up considerable expertise. The Soviets were interested in oil but also in expanding their empire, securing a warm water port, establishing a string of Soviet puppet buffer states on its southern border, and making sure its own sizable Muslim minorities were not influenced by the rising Islamic fundamentalism in Iran and other countries. During the long Cold War, the Middle East was one of the hottest areas where the United States and the USSR faced off. And then, when the Soviet Union collapsed in 1991, the United States was truly left as the only outside power in the region. Previously, the United States and the Soviets had each "policed" their own respective client states and that had maintained a certain order in an otherwise chaotic area; now the United States was left as the region's sole policeman, with all the costs on our part and rising resentments on the side of the Arab states that implied.

Change had, meanwhile, been inexorably occurring in the internal politics and societies of the Middle East that also affected the international situation. First came the rise of Pan-Arabism, largely led by Gamel Abdul Nasser of Egypt in its early years, a movement that sought to find common ground and common policies among all the Arab states. Concurrently, second, came the rise of Arab nationalism, socialism, and the secular, Baath political parties that governed for a time in the 1950s, 1960s, and 1970s. Meanwhile, third, social change was occurring in the Arab world, including the rise of a middle class and the growing impatience for change coupled with religious fundamentalism of the Arab masses. Fourth came the Iranian revolution of 1979, the rise of Islamic fundamentalism, and the growing popularity of the idea of a distinct Islamic model of change and development. Finally, the rising and continued demand for Middle East oil on the part of Europe, the United States, Japan, and now China enabled some Islamic countries to become fabulously rich, while other nonoil countries remained poor and the gaps between rich and poor both between and within states continued to widen.

This history helps provide us with the background and context for discussing today's Middle East and the manifold and dangerous problems that confront U.S. policy there. Among them are the following:

- The continuing and festering Israel-Palestinian conflict that if unresolved will continue to foster violence, conflict, and war.
- Rising Islamic fundamentalism in North Africa and throughout the Middle East that is very dangerous for U.S. interests.
- The war in Iraq: as the United States pulls out, there is no assurance that Iraq will not explode again in violence and civil war.
- The war in Afghanistan, presently going badly, and which may result in a Taliban-controlled Afghanistan.
- The war against Al Qaeda, currently concentrated in Pakistan, complicated by the impenetrability of the country's northwest border territories, by the high stakes of nuclear weapons present, and by the fact Pakistan sees its interests in a different light than does the United States.
- The rising threat of terrorism and Islamic fundamentalism in such oil-rich countries as Saudi Arabia, Kuwait, Bahrain, and the UAE; if these countries go down, the entire economies of Europe, the United States, and Japan will collapse.
- The presence of a nuclear capacity in Iran, which may give that country the long-sought "Islamic bomb" and trigger an attack by Israel or by the United States, or renewed general conflagration in the Middle East and beyond.
- The potential for violent instability in Central Asia, Georgia, and the Caucasus, another area rich in oil and natural gas that we and Europe are counting on as an alternative to unsettled and conflict-prone Persian Gulf oil, but which the Russians see as part of "Greater Russia."
- The triumph of Hezbollah in Lebanon and Hamas in Gaza signals a more violent, more militant form of Islamic fundamentalism capable of actually coming to power.

There we have it: a region, perhaps more than any other, likely to explode in conflict and war, including nuclear war, and in which the stakes for the United States (oil, stability, security, our economy, Israel) could not be higher. In the next section we will be looking at some of the country-specific and regional hot spots within the area.

Individual Countries and Subregions

Egypt

Egypt, along with India, China, Indonesia, Pakistan, Brazil, and Mexico, has long been considered one of the most important countries in the Third World. With a population of seventy-five million, it is the most populous country in the Middle East, commands the entrance to the Nile River as well as the Suez Canal, and is a candidate for a permanent UN Security Council seat. According to a saying, as goes Egypt, so goes (much of) the Middle East.

Egypt has a long and glorious history: the pharaohs, the pyramids, one of the cradles of civilization in the valley of the Nile. It is a relatively new nation (since 1953) but a very ancient culture and civilization. Its influence in ancient history reached easterly into the Sinai desert and beyond, along North Africa, into the islands of the Mediterranean, and even across the Mediterranean—although some European countries are reluctant to admit that because of Egypt's African influence. Later, it was subjected to repeated interventions, invasions, and foreign occupations: Greece, Rome, Mesopotamia, Iran, Mongols, Turks, eventually France and Great Britain.

With a per capita income of $5,400, Egypt is classified as a lower-middle-income country. It is not among the Middle East's oil-wealthy nations. Its population is too large for the size of its territory (effectively limited to the Nile River Valley; the rest is desert), and jobs and economic growth are not keeping up with population increase. Meanwhile, social pressures—rapid urbanization, high unemployment, a youthful population, a growing middle class, Islamic fundamentalism—are all building up. Egypt is one of those key countries listed earlier that could explode in social or political revolution.

Politically, Egypt was led by Hosni Mubarak. He was an authoritarian leader, a former military officer, not very much inclined toward democracy and human rights, and nearing the end of his life. However, for a long time he had maintained order and stability, traits that we also value. The great fear at the policy level is that after Mubarak, Egypt will explode in revolution, chaos, or civil war. Both the Islamic and the secular opposition to the regime is growing, although religious fundamentalism is becoming dominant.

Egypt is important for many reasons. First is its strategic location in the eastern Mediterranean and along the Suez Canal and Red Sea. Second, it is a big country; if Egypt falls into chaos or the fundamentalists gain control, it is a really big deal. Third, Egypt has long maintained a peaceful border and more-or-less normal diplomatic relations with Israel, but there are both internal and external pressures to abandon that position. Fourth, Egypt is one of the largest recipients in the world of U.S. aid; if that aid fails to achieve its goals of Middle East peace, it will represent a terrible failure of U.S. policy. Finally, and related to the previous point, Egypt is essential to the success of a future Palestinian state; if Egypt's support for a moderate solution to the Israeli-Palestine peace process is withdrawn, the entire project is likely to fail.

Iran

Iran is another of those important countries that we need to worry about a lot. With a population of seventy-one million, vast resources including oil, and lying astride all the Middle East's main east-west and north-south trade, travel, and strategic routes, Iran is a country of large and vital interests. In earlier decades, through the 1970s, Iran was not just a partner of the United States but we saw it as an important regional power capable of keeping the Soviet Union at bay and maintaining peace and stability throughout the oil-rich, all-important Persian Gulf area. But since 1979, with its Islamic-fundamentalist revolution, Iran has turned hostile to the United States, and now with its efforts to build nuclear capability, including nuclear bombs, Iran has the capacity to destabilize the entire area.

Iran has, like Egypt, a long and glorious history as a civilization but a relatively short one (since 1906) as an independent nation-state. It is a proud nation, fiercely independent, its people having long resisted outside invasions. The Iranian plateau could be said to occupy the center of the Middle East; it also borders on troublesome Armenia,

Azerbaijan, Turkmenistan, and Central Asia, and (across the Caspian Sea) Russia; it lies between and shares long borders with the two countries in which the United States is at war: Iraq and Afghanistan. Iran's per capita income is twice that of Egypt's and at least that much in comparison with its immediate neighbors; it is a well-educated country, very sophisticated, and with a large middle class. Perhaps the most important things to remember about Iran are: (i) it is Persian rather than Arab and very proud of that difference, and (ii) it speaks Farsi and not Arabic. These features set Iran off as different from all its neighbors.

From a comparative politics point of view, Iran was the first of the Middle East countries to have a revolution ushering in a fundamentalist Islamic regime. Excitingly, though we may not approve of the revolution's excesses and many of its policies, Iran nevertheless represents an effort to build a genuinely Islamic state, to develop an indigenous or homegrown model of politics, society, and development; and it serves as an example and inspiration to other countries. For good or ill, Iran may represent the future of the Middle East.

All these factors make Iran an extremely important country, in these terms the most important in the Middle East. Then if we add in Iran's nuclear program the Israeli threat to bomb and destroy these facilities, the pressures in the United States for us to do the bombing if the Israelis do not, and the possibilities that such actions could set off a general Middle Eastern conflagration that would destroy the Saudi and Persian Gulf oil fields and destabilize the entire area, we have a truly worrisome situation. Iran may well be the most important, and at the same time the most complex and the most volatile, of all the foreign policy problems with which the United States must deal.

Iraq-Afghanistan

Iraq and Afghanistan are two very different countries. But because they are linked in the eyes of the public and in U.S. strategic policy, we will treat them here under a single heading.

The United States militarily invaded and occupied Iraq in the aftermath of the 9/11 attacks on the World Trade Center and the Pentagon. This was done (i) to get a measure of revenge and satisfaction for those acts of terrorism, (ii) because we thought Iraq's ruling dictator, Saddam Hussein, was developing weapons of mass destruction (WMDs), and (iii) as part of President George W. Bush's and his neoconservative advisers' unrealistic campaign to, hopefully, bring democracy and freedom to the Middle East. The terrible mistakes and miscalculations of that campaign are well known: there were no WMDs; the terrorists of 9/11 had almost nothing to do with Iraq; we helped destroy the only institutions (army, police, bureaucracy, majority party) that might have held Iraq together; we were completely unprepared for the anti-American insurgency that developed; we had no thought-out exit strategy, and our nation-building and democracy-promotion efforts in Iraq were generally inept.

We will be rehashing these issues for a long time; perhaps now what we should concentrate on is future strategy: where do we do from here? Almost no one believes anymore that we can create a pure or a Jeffersonian democracy in Iraq. The question's now are: can we sustain an elected, middle-of-the-road, and reasonably competent government in Iraq; can that government prevent chaos and full-scale civil war from developing between Shia, Sunni, and Kurds; can that government keep the Al Qaeda terrorists at bay; and can that government maintain stability long enough (let us say, five years) for us to withdraw with some degree of honor, avoiding the debacle that followed the U.S. defeat and retreat from Vietnam, while also giving Iraq at least a shot at a stable and democratic future? Betting on those very large stakes, President Barack Obama has vowed to end the war in Iraq and bring our troops home—except that, instead of coming home, many of these troops are being transferred to the Afghanistan war.

Afghanistan is a much poorer, much less institutionalized, more violent, more primitive, more tribal society, with a far smaller middle class than Iraq. On several indices, Afghanistan is ranked only above Somalia among the 193 nations in the world as the least governable. The chances of succeeding at democracy-promotion and nation-building in Afghanistan are far lower than in Iraq, about the same odds as winning the lottery. You cannot base a sound policy on such low odds. You need either to give up and withdraw our troops from Afghanistan, leaving jet fighters and missiles to prevent Afghanistan from becoming a base for terrorist attacks on the United States, or you need to change the strategy. President Obama, for now, has opted for the latter tactic.

The issue is also bound up in America's domestic politics. Obama said during the campaign that he intended to pull out of Iraq, but if he now withdraws from Afghanistan too, it will confirm the public's long-held belief that Democrats are weak on defense. And that will likely cost the Democrats seats in the next election. So Obama is stuck: if he goes in deeper, he will draw the wrath of the large antiwar wing of the Democratic Party; if he withdraws, he loses congressional seats and maybe sacrifices his own reelection possibilities.

Meanwhile, the war itself is going badly. More American troops are dying. The Taliban controls up to 80 percent of the national territory. Democracy-promotion and nation-building are not working well. The government is precarious and the U.S. and NATO armed forces lack a plan. We have not yet captured Osama bin Laden who may be holed up in those impenetrable mountains of northwest Pakistan. At the same time, the fighting, bombing, and dying are now shifting to Pakistan whose own government is also under siege. But Pakistan's government (i) has nuclear weapons that could fall into the hands of Islamist radicals, and (ii) for nationalistic reasons, does not want U.S. military forces in its territory.

What to do? None of the options looks good. We can't stay there indefinitely because both our resources and the public's patience are wearing thin. But we can't withdraw either, certainly not precipitously, because the consequences of a full Taliban/Al Queda takeover of Afghanistan, and maybe Pakistan, too, are frightening: more violence, more conflict, more militant Islamic fundamentalism, more terrorist attacks on us and our allies.

It's a tough call but I've reached my own conclusions, which readers are free to disagree with. Lacking the language skills, the cultural empathy, and the necessary knowledge of Afghan society, I don't think we can succeed or win in Afghanistan. We can't win militarily and, given the country's low socioeconomic and institutional level, we can't succeed at nation- or democracy-building either. You can't build stability and democracy in countries that lack the cultural, social, economic, or governmental foundations for it. And if we can't win and we can't succeed with the current policy, we need a new policy that does work or else we need to get out. Hopefully, via air power, drones, and CIA machinations, we could then from a distance prevent those worst-case scenarios of the previous paragraph from coming to pass.

Israel-Palestine

The Israel-Palestine conflict is one of the most vexing and complicated issues in U.S. foreign policy. It is complicated for a number of reasons: (i) the issue is intimately caught up in U.S. domestic politics; (ii) conditions within both Israel and Palestine, as well as in the broader Middle East, keep changing; and (iii) the issue has the potential to set off a general Middle East war and conflagration.

Superficially, the issue looks like it is easily resolvable: the two-state solution. Under that approach, Israel's security would be assured and the Palestinians, long stateless, would get a state of their own, consisting of the West Bank and Gaza. The borders that existed before the 1967 war would be restored. Jerusalem would be divided between the two, and the Golan Heights would be demilitarized. It all sounds easy. Peace in the Middle East!

But now things get complicated. First, any American administration that deals with this issue must reckon with the power of the Israeli lobby, the most powerful foreign affairs lobby in the United States. The Israeli lobby does not take kindly to any criticism of, let alone pressure on, Israel. The lobby can mobilize immense amounts of votes, pressure, and money, to say nothing of the charge of anti-Semitism, against anyone who votes against Israel or seeks to force a solution on it against Israeli interests. Congressmen are scared stiff of the Israeli lobby, knowing that any vote against it is likely the kiss of death for the congressman's reelection possibilities. Even President Barack Obama, in pursuit of the two-state solution, after telling Israel to stop building new Jewish settlements in the West Bank, was forced to backtrack on his statement. The word on the street in Washington is: *never* buck the power of the Israeli lobby.

The second factor to consider is that conditions within both Israel and the Palestinian territories keep changing, with negative consequences for the peace process. In Palestine, the generally peaceful and accommodating Arab Christians have been driven out, going from 25 percent to 2 percent of the Arab population, leaving the territories in control of the more radical Islamic fundamentalist elements, the Palestinian Liberation Organization and Hamas. We should also note that the population of the Arabs is increasing much faster than population growth rates in Israel.

In Israel, there have also been major changes domestically. For a long time Israeli politics was dominated by European or Ashquenazi Jews, who were more reasonable and accommodating on the Palestine issue. Then in the 1970s, because of Jewish immigration from the Arab countries (Sephardic Jews) and Russia, Israeli politics became more conservative and hard-line toward the Arabs. These Jews tended to hate the Arabs and were unwilling to compromise with them; in addition, they believed that the main Arab or West Bank territories were the ancient lands of Samaria and Judea that God Himself had given to the Israelites. How can you urge compromise on someone who believes his recalcitrant policies derive from the word of God? Politically in Israel, this shift was reflected in the declining power of the Labor (Ashquenazi) Party and the rising power of the Likud Party, of which the current prime minister, Benjamin Netanyahu, is the representative. In short, changing demographics and politics are pushing both Palestinian and Israeli officials into more extreme positions that are almost impossible to compromise.

The issue now has the potential to set off a full-scale regional conflagration, which is why the United States must worry about it. First, the Israeli state has over the years become a more militarized and armed state, including (by best estimates) over two hundred nuclear weapons that the Israelis, if attacked, surrounded, and cornered by the far more numerous Arabs, would probably not hesitate to use. Second, with the takeover of Gaza and much of the Palestinian government by Hamas, and of much of neighboring (to the north) Lebanon by the even more treacherous Hezbollah, Israel faces the prospect—and even the reality—of terrorist attacks, bombings, and shellings within its own territory and along and across its northern border.

Third, Israel's Arab neighbors, still often dedicated to the destruction of Israel, are getting stronger all the time, in terms of population, economic wealth, and military capacity. That is why revolutionary Iran's building of a nuclear weapons capacity is so dangerous from Israel's point of view and that of the United States. Because if Iran has nuclear weapons, it might be able to attack Israel with them or use them to neutralize Israel's current nuclear advantage. Neutralization of Israel's nukes might then enable the Arab states to attack and overwhelm Israel on the ground where they have the advantage: sheer population numbers. On the other hand, if the United States or Israel seek to preempt Iran's nuclear program by bombing it to smithereens, that could set off a general Middle Eastern conflagration that could destabilize Kuwait, Saudi Arabia, and the other Persian Gulf states on which we, Europe, and Asia are absolutely dependent for our oil.

What to do? Can I confess that in this situation I don't know what to do, meanwhile recognizing that the issue may be outside of our ability to determine the outcome. About all we can do is to keep urging both Israelis and Palestinians to keep talking, be reasonable, see if they, with our help, can work out the differences. The two-state solution still seems the best bet even while its prospects seem dimmer than a few years ago. We need to try to keep the Israelis from acting precipitously (e.g., bombing Iran), while also putting pressure on Iran to curtail its nuclear program. But there is declining faith in the world, and in the U.S. government, that these policies will work. Meanwhile, the prospect that the Israel-Palestine and, more generally, the Israel-Middle East conflict could spin out of control is gaining currency. It is a very dangerous situation.

Central Asia

Central Asia is a brand new area for study. The five new republics (Kazakhstan, Kyrgys Republic, Tajikistan, Turkmenistan, and Uzbekistan) that make up Central Asia, plus Armenia, Azerbaijan, and the Trans Caucasus, were once part of the Soviet Union; since the early 1990s, as the Soviet Union disintegrated, they have become independent states. In this sense, Central Asia is like the Baltic countries (Estonia, Latvia, Lithuania): similarly once a part of the Soviet Union, now independent, and with interesting, comparable similarities as well as differences between them. These "new" areas offer wonderful opportunities for specialization for young scholars and policy analysts precisely because they are so new and there are few persons specializing in them. You can practically create your own area studies program all to yourself.[1]

Since Central Asia was for a long time part of the Soviet Union, it is not usually considered a part of the Middle East, even though it shares many cultural and religious features with the Middle Eastern countries. Nor, since it is now independent, can it any longer be thought of as part of Greater Russia; culturally, ethnically, and religiously, it is quite different from Slavic or European Russia. Though it borders on China's western frontier, it is not really a part of Asia as are the countries considered in the previous chapter, and it falls outside of the South Asian regional focus as well. So with all these differences, we will have to consider Central Asia as a new area unto itself, but with important links to the Middle East.

Historically, all the countries along the southern rim of Russia and just north of Iran and the Middle Eastern heartland had, culturally, socially, and religiously, been for many centuries part of or dependent on the Middle East. This is the area that lies on the shores of the Caspian Sea stretching eastward all the way to China. The Mongols, Persia, Russia, and China all had, at one time or another, contributed to the ethnic and cultural makeup of the area. However, the greatest influence came from the Turks who had migrated southward toward Central Asia and westward toward present-day Turkey from the Asian steppes. For centuries, most of this area had been dominated by three Islamic-Turkish states.

In the nineteenth century, as Russia under the czars expanded its territory toward the south, Central Asia and the Trans Caucasus came under Russian control. After the Russian Revolution in 1917, the Soviet Union consolidated and expanded its role in this area. The fierce and often violent independence of these territories was subjugated to Soviet-communist control.

When the Soviet Union collapsed in 1991, all these territories of the Trans Caucasus and Central Asia became independent. None of them was well prepared for independence. They lacked institutions, functioning governments, or a political culture supportive of democracy. In this sense, they were like the Baltics or Eastern Europe after they also received independence from the USSR—except that Central Asia and the Trans Caucasus were far poorer and less developed than these others. Lacking democratic institutions and a firm socioeconomic base, most of the countries continued under a form of communist and authoritarian government that was not much different from what they had experienced under the Soviets.

If one goes back before Russian rule, however, all of these countries had been powerfully shaped by their proximity to, and the culture and civilization of, the Middle East. Of the new states of the area, two were majority-Christian—Armenia and Georgia—but they had also been profoundly influenced by their exposure over the centuries to Muslim Persia and Turkey. The other countries, Azerbaijan and the five Central Asian countries of Tajikistan, Kazakhstan, Uzbekistan, Kyrgyzstan, and Turkmenistan, were majority-Muslim and had been strongly influenced by a full millennium of Middle Eastern culture. Tajikistan was predominantly Persian in culture and language, while the others were more Turkish culturally and ethnically.

A new Cold War is shaping up in this area, which could be profoundly dangerous in the future. None of these countries has a stable government. Georgia is the only democracy in the area, and its government is also shaky. Russia, though weakened after the collapse of the Soviet Union, still thinks of this area, like the Baltics, as part of "Greater Russia" and recently sent troops into Georgia to encourage its breakaway provinces of Ossetia and Abkhazia to rejoin with Russia. The United States and Europe also have strong interests in this area, in part because of the military bases (to assist in the wars in Iraq and Afghanistan) we have established there and, in part, because of vast fields of oil and natural gas that, especially in Europe, are seen as an alternative source from a Russia that uses its gas and oil to extract political and strategic concessions from its neighbors. Meanwhile, from the south and the Islamic world, Iran and its agents are meddling in the Caucasus and Central Asia and seeking to foment their brand of Islamic fundamentalism.

It looks as though the Caucasus and Central Asia will be unstable and volatile for many years to come, not only because of their own institutional and developmental weaknesses but also because a variety of outside powers are and will continue meddling in their internal affairs. To this dangerous set of influences we must add the fact that the Central Asian countries were among the places where, during the Cold War, the Soviets had positioned nuclear weapons and launch cites. While the United States and its allies have worked hard to control and get a handle on these weapons, some of these remain under the control of local authorities or have been sold to third parties on the private market—what we irreverently call "loose nukes."

Turkey

Turkey is the second largest of the Middle Eastern states in population (seventy-four million) but not in size. There is even some doubt as to whether we should classify Turkey as Middle Eastern. First, it is ethnically Turkish and not Arab. Second, while it is predominantly Islamic, it practices a generally milder and less fundamentalist form of Islam; officially, Turkey is a secular state. Third, Turkey has one foot in Europe—in more ways than one.

To begin, although Turkey's territory is mostly in Asia Minor, a small part of its territory lies across the Bosporus waterway in what has traditionally been considered Europe. Also, Turkey is a member of NATO, the North Atlantic Treaty Organization, and is a leading candidate for membership in the European Union (EU), although its size, relative poverty (one-third the European level but considerably higher than most countries of the Middle East), and Muslim background make that problematic. In addition, Turkey is, along with Lebanon, the most Western of the Middle Eastern countries in terms of its thinking, culture, and parliamentary government. The most Western parts of Turkey are in and around Istanbul; as one travels farther east, however, the country becomes (i) poorer, (ii) less Western, and (iii) more Islamic and "Middle Eastern."

Turkey provides a bridge, not only across the Bosporus but also across the continents between Europe and Asia, between East and West. Which way it eventually leans (or, most likely, both ways) is tremendously important. Long seen as a crossroads and occupying a strategic location, Turkey has historically been buffeted about in international crosswinds. Mesopotamia, Persia, Greece, Rome, the Mongols, and eventually Turkish tribes originating in Asian Russia have all successively conquered the territory that is today's Turkey. There are spectacular Greek and Roman ruins in Turkey, and Christians will recall that Saint Paul visited and wrote a number of his biblical epistles to the churches of what was then Asia Minor. Constantinople, now renamed Istanbul, was for a thousand years the capital of Byzantium and the center of the Eastern (Christian) Orthodox Church; after 1453 it became the capital of the Ottoman or Turkish (Muslim) empire until it collapsed in World War I. There is a lot of history in this part of the world.

Turkey is a crucial country, big and important. It has long been a U.S. and NATO ally, though recently, because of U.S. inattention, the war in Iraq, and U.S. policy in the Middle East more generally, that alliance has been strained. Turkey's allegiance to the West would also be strengthened if its application to join the EU were speedily accepted, but European publics are worried about having a big, poor, Islamic, at least semi-Middle Eastern country within their ranks, and all the trouble that might cause. Europeans fear Turkish immigrants will take their jobs, change their culture, and add to their terrorist worries, and that Turkey's membership might drag them into Middle Eastern conflicts peripheral to their interests.

When Turkey is rebuffed by Europe, it reacts by emphasizing its eastern connections. Those include borders and/or relations with Syria, Iraq, Iran, and, interestingly, Israel. But it also includes Turkey's reaching out to the big, important, and oil-rich Central Asian republics which, recall, have strong ethnic Turkish cultural and linguistic connections and which Turkey sees as a major target of its economic, political, and energy policies. In short, Turkey has an eastern policy as well as a western policy, and we would do well by assuring it stays in the western camp even while it serves as a moderating force in the Middle East and Central Asia.

Conclusion

It's likely that other areas of the world are more important for U.S. foreign policy than the Middle East. East Asia and Europe, East and West, come to mind. And on an everyday basis, because of immigration, Latin America has more capacity to affect us in our daily lives than any other area.

The Middle East, however, is today probably the most dangerous and volatile of all world areas. War, revolution, terrorism, even nuclear war could all break out at any time. Think of Iraq, Afghanistan, Iran, Pakistan, Central Asia, Egypt, Saudi Arabia, Morocco, Libya, Tunisia, Syria, Lebanon, Jordan, Yemen, the Israeli-Palestinian conflict—all or several or a combination of these could explode at any moment. Now add in the fact that the United States and the other industrialized countries—Japan, Western Europe—are all absolutely dependent on Middle Eastern oil for jobs, industry, and the health of our economies, all of which could quickly go down the drain if one or two of the countries listed earlier exploded in revolution, conflict, or civil war, and the oil were cut off. Then add in nuclear weapons—in Israel, Pakistan, Iran, and perhaps other countries, too. In any one of several scenarios, trouble in the Middle East could easily escalate into a region-wide, maybe even global conflagration.

And the trouble is that we can do little to affect the outcome. Quite a number of these conflicts are out of our control, beyond our capacity to influence them more than marginally. Again, think of Iran's nuclear weapons, the war in Afghanistan, the Israel-Palestine conflict, possible revolution in Saudi Arabia and other oil-producing states. How much can we change these things? Not very much. Now add in demographic change, social change, geography, and resource "haves" versus "have nots"—things that we cannot change at all and that themselves have the capacity to destabilize the area.

Obviously we want a stable and reliable (for purpose of oil supplies) Middle East. That means we should help the Middle East, especially the poor countries, with economic development, building infrastructure, and expanding civil society. We can help with literacy programs, education, and building universities, including university exchange programs. We can also help the Middle East with human rights improvements through modernization of the police, courts, and judiciary. Additionally, we can help with governance issues and the building of strong and effective institutions that can deliver effective social and economic programs. But at this stage we should not vigorously push democracy promotion in the Middle East. First, much of the Middle East, lacking the prerequisites, such as a strong middle class, is not yet ready for democracy. And second, by advocating too actively for democracy, we may well destabilize the very countries we depend on so heavily for oil, which are the last countries in the world we would want to see destabilized.

Former secretary of state George Shultz once told the author that he had to *fight* to keep the Middle East from taking 100 percent of his time. On the one hand, Shultz's comment, only slightly exaggerated, tells us how little time is left over for dealing with other important countries, regions, and issues. On the other, his comment suggests also how difficult, intractable, and dangerous this area is to American and even global international relations.

Note

1. In the early-to-mid-1990s, I was teaching at the National War College in Washington, D.C., at the highest rung (master's degree level) in the Defense Department's Professional Military Education (PME) Program. This was just at the time the Soviet Union was disintegrating and the Central Asian countries were becoming independent. The Defense Department recognized Central Asia's importance for energy and strategic purposes but, since it was a new area, DOD had no one with that particular regional expertise. So it plucked out a young woman whose previous expertise was Latin America, who did not know the languages, culture, history sociology, or politics of Central Asia, and told her "You are now our expert on Central Asia."

Suggested Readings

Ahmad, Leila. *Women and Gender in Islam* (New Haven: Yale University Press, 1992).

Bill, James A. and Robert Springborg. *Politics in the Middle East* (New York: Harper Collins, 1990).

Enayati, Hamid. *Modern Islamic Political Thought* (Austin, TX: University of Texas Press, 1982).

Esposito, John. *Islam and Politics* (Syracuse: Syracuse University Press, 1987).

Fisher, Sidney N. *The Middle East: A History* (New York: Knopf, 1979).

Hudson, Michael. *Arab Politics* (New Haven, CT: Yale University Press, 1977).

Hunter, Shereen and Hama Malik (eds.). *Modernization, Democracy, and Islam* (Westport, CT: Praeger, 2005).

Lewis, Bernard. *Islam and the West* (New York: Oxford University Press, 1993).

Noll, John. *Islam* (Boulder, CO: Westview, 1982).

Pinault, David. *The Shiites* (New York: St. Martin's, 1992).

Pipes, Daniel. *In the Path of God: Islam and Political Power* (New York: Basic Books, 1983).

CHAPTER 7

Latin America

Latin America, along with sub-Saharan Africa, is the most neglected area in the world from the point of view of U.S, foreign policy. Almost no one in Washington, D.C., pays serious attention to Latin America. Europe, Asia, Russia, and the Middle East all have higher priority; Latin America is low on the totem pole of U.S. attention. Few policymakers or the public, for that matter, pay sustained attention to developments in the Western hemisphere; few have ever lived or traveled there; and we certainly do not think of Latin America as drawing concentrated serious policy attention. As former *New York Times* columnist James "Scotty" Reston once wrote, "The United States will do anything for Latin America—give foreign aid, send the Peace Corps, initiate the Alliance for Progress—except read about it."

U.S. practices toward Latin America indicate what may be called "benign neglect"—and sometimes, when we militarily intervene in the area, it is not so benign. That is, we largely ignore the area until some big crisis, like the Cuban revolution, forces it onto our agenda. Then we respond frantically and often inappropriately since we have no long-term policy toward the area. Much of the history of U.S. foreign policy toward Latin America can be written in terms of the alternation between neglect and frantic intervention.

At the heart of the U.S. response, or the lack thereof, to Latin America are deep-seated prejudices about the area. The United States has long been a Protestant country and Latin America is Catholic; the United States is a colonial product of progressive Great Britain and the Netherlands while Latin America is a product of long-regressive Spain and Portugal; the United States is a successful country while Latin America has long been weak and unstable. Fundamentally, we do not believe Latin America has the capacity to govern itself or to see to its own successful economic development; therefore, we must rush in from time to time to put out brush fires and rescue the area, mainly from its own ineptness.

Historically, Latin America has always been portrayed in the United States as comic-opera: unstable, with frequent revolutions, with comical and incapable leaders, full of bearded revolutionaries and violent narco-traffickers. Along with all these other prejudices, there are class and racial prejudices: about the only Latin Americans we ever see in our towns and cities in the United States are those from the lower classes, often illiterate and uneducated, very often illegal immigrants, who are also brown, black, and of a mixed racial background. Though no one says this publicly or in polite company, racial and ethnic prejudices play strong roles in U.S. policy toward the region: we just don't believe the Latinos are "up to it."

All this is sad and tragic not only morally but also from a U.S. policy point of view, for Latin America should by all logic be a natural partner for the United States. Look at a map: we share the Western hemisphere with Latin America, we have a long, common border with the area, and as relatively "new" (two hundred years, plus or minus) nations we have much in common. Both the United States and Latin America want a peaceful, democratic, and prosperous Western hemisphere; we both want to keep out terrorists and hostile foreign powers; and we have a strong interest in working together to achieve those goals.

The United States and Latin America are complementary in many ways. That alone should serve as a basis for good and mutually cooperative relations. We are a high-tech society while Latin America has an abundance of hand labor. We are, still, a manufacturing and an industrialized nation while Latin America has vast mineral and agricultural resources. Our economies and societies are closely complementary. We are both products of a Western tradition and hold dear many of the same values, including a strong commitment to democracy and human rights, even while culturally we are the offspring of two different Western traditions, the one mainly Anglo-Saxon and the other mainly Hispanic. For all these reasons, the United States and Latin America should be allies and natural trading partners.

The United States and Latin America are also mutually interdependent. Not only do we share that long and porous two-thousand-mile border with Mexico, but we also have an even longer water "border," around the Gulf of Mexico and up the Florida coast, with the nations of the Caribbean. On a host of issues the United States and Latin America are interconnected. It is not well known that Mexico is our second-largest trading partner, behind only Canada but ahead of both China and Japan; other Latin American countries (Brazil, Colombia, Venezuela, Peru) are in the top thirty. We get abundant oil and natural gas from Latin America (Venezuela, Mexico, Ecuador), and we sell U.S.-manufactured goods there. American tourists go to Latin America in vast and increasing numbers, while Latin America provides us with an abundant and hardworking labor supply. Food supplies, water resources, especially in the American Southwest, and, let's face it, drugs are other areas in which the United States and Latin America are interdependent: our demand fuels their production. Music, dance, food, and culture, in general, no longer are respecters of borders. In all these and many other areas there are abundant grounds for peaceful and cooperative relations.

Latin America is also ignored by the United States because, unlike Iran, North Korea, Iraq, China, or Afghanistan, it does not seem to constitute a threat to U.S. interests. Argentina and Brazil gave up their nuclear programs some years ago; Latin America is not a training ground or haven for terrorists bent on attacking the United States, nor are any of the Latin American states about to invade the U.S. militarily. The absence of a serious threat in that region makes it easier to put Latin America's not-quite-so-pressing issues on the back burner.

Some Latin Americans now lament that they gave up their nuclear programs, not that they want or need nuclear weapons but because then the United States would surely pay more attention to them. Others say, only half facetiously, that they could use a few more Fidel Castros (Does Venezuela's Hugo Chávez now fill that role?) because that also attracts U.S. attention. Most recently the U.S. Department of Defense has "discovered" Mexico, not because they are particularly interested in Mexico but because of heightened levels of violence, drug trafficking, and the potential of it becoming a failed state right on the

U.S. border. Instability in Mexico is now perceived as a "threat" to U.S. interests.

And that gets us to our final introductory point regarding Latin America. U.S. foreign policy is threat-oriented. Absent a serious threat, we don't pay attention to this or any other region. As Colin Powell used to say when he was secretary of state, "I wake up every morning and I already have forty-seven major problems on my plate. The last thing I need to think about is a forty-eighth."

But precisely therein lies a problem, with particular relevance for Latin America and sub-Saharan Africa. U.S. policy is threat-oriented (the Cold War, now the war on terrorism). Without a threat, we do not pay serious attention. But in the Latin American case, what we need, given the vast resources, the history of good relations, and our mutual interdependence with the region, is a policy that is opportunity-oriented, not just threat-based. In Latin America we have the opportunity, now that the Cold War is over and there is no serious or imminent threat emanating from the area, to put our relations on this more-positive, optimistic, cooperative basis, as distinct from the conflicts and misunderstandings of the past. But whether we will seize that opportunity, or even if that "full platter" of which Secretary Powell spoke affords us the time to even think about it, is another matter. But if we do not, both we and Latin America will be the losers.

Social and Economic Development

The countries of Latin America occupy an intermediary position in our rankings of global social and economic development. Latin America is neither as affluent as North America, Western Europe, or Japan and the Four Tigers, nor as poor as sub-Saharan Africa, Southeast Asia, and the nonoil countries of the Middle East.

If we take a long-term perspective going back half a century to the 1960s, Latin America has not done altogether badly in achieving development. Over this period, among the world's developing areas, Latin America ranks second only to East Asia in terms of economic growth. In this regard, Latin America is ahead of both the Middle East and sub-Saharan Africa. Latin America, with the exception of Brazil, has not experienced the miracle growth rates of East Asia, but, with growth of 3–5 percent or more per year for many countries, it has not done altogether badly either.

As table 7.1 shows, of the twenty Latin American countries, ten or half of them are now in the UMC or upper-middle-income category with per capita income between $3,706 and $11,955 per year. That is a remarkable accomplishment over a fifty-year period. Quite a number of Latin American countries—Argentina, Brazil, Chile, Costa Rica, Mexico, Panama, Uruguay, Venezuela—are poised on the threshold of becoming high-income countries. Of the remaining ten countries in the list, nine of them are now in the lower-middle-income (LMC) category. That leaves only one country, Haiti, in the lower-income category.

As these figures indicate, while much of Latin America is still poor by comparison with North America or Western Europe, it is not

Table 7.1 Latin American per capita income

Country	Per capita income (in $)	Category
Argentina	6,050	UMC
Bolivia	1,260	LMC
Brazil	5,910	UMC
Chile	8,350	UMC
Colombia	3,250	LMC
Costa Rica	5,560	UMC
Cuba	–	UMC
Dominican Republic	3,550	LMC
Ecuador	3,080	LMC
El Salvador	2,850	LMC
Guatemala	2,440	LMC
Haiti	560	LIC
Honduras	1,600	LMC
Mexico	8,340	UMC
Nicaragua	980	LMC
Panama	5,510	UMC
Paraguay	1,670	LMC
Peru	3,450	LMC
Uruguay	6,380	UMC
Venezuela	7,323	UMC

UMC: Upper middle income country; LMC: Lower middle income country.

nearly as poor as it once was. Latin America has largely broken out of its earlier situation of absolute poverty and joined the ranks of truly developing nations. In almost every country of Latin America, absolute poverty has been reduced, in some countries quite dramatically. You can still see heart-wrenching poverty in Latin America, but now we are talking mainly about pockets of poverty rather than a society-wide culture of poverty. A careful look at the numbers reveals that of all the global areas treated here, Latin America ranks closest to Eastern Europe in its level of economic development. That Latin America is reaching European levels, even if it is poorer Eastern Europe, is quite an accomplishment.

Per capita income figures are averages, however; they tell us nothing about how the income is distributed. And by this measure Latin America does not come out so well: it has the worst distribution of income, in terms of the wide gaps between rich and poor, of any area in the world. In this regard, Latin America stands in striking contrast to East Asia where phenomenal economic growth rates have been accompanied by a remarkably even distribution of the new wealth. Not so in Latin America where, as development proceeded, the gaps between the wealthy and poor elements in society widened rather than narrowed. By this measure, Latin America is closer to the oil-rich Middle Eastern countries.

To sum up this section: Latin America has achieved impressive economic growth over the past half century, lifting the continent out of its earlier poverty. But that growth has been uneven and the distribution of the new wealth has also been uneven.

Background

Though an offshoot of the Western tradition, Latin America's history is very different from that of the United States. The United States was, in its thirteen original colonies, a product of Northern Europe, of Great Britain and the Netherlands, of Protestantism, the capitalist revolution, an independent middle class, and the modernity of the seventeenth century. Latin America, in contrast, founded a full century earlier, was a product of medievalism, of feudalism, of Spain and Portugal, of Catholicism, of absolutism, and of a rigid class-caste system that persists to this day. The United States was "born free," in the sense that it never had a feudal past (except in the slave-holding South) with all its attendant social-racial rigidities and hierarchies, while Latin America was "born feudal," a product of the Middle Ages. The last vestiges of feudalism in the United States were blown away in the Civil War (*Gone With the Wind*, as the title of Margaret Mitchell's famous book and movie puts it) enabling the entire nation to become modern, while Latin America remained locked in the grip of a feudal past that prevented modernization.

The basic institutions that Spain and Portugal established in the New World and their contrasts with the United States are summarized in table 7.2. Thus, the Latin American political tradition was authoritarian and absolutist; the economy, statist and mercantilist; and the society, feudal and two-class. The Roman Catholic Church was similarly absolutist and top-down, while intellectual life, legal training, and the educational system were scholastic, deductive, and based on rote memorization. In contrast, the North American tradition, founded a full century later, by which time the hold of feudal institutions had been largely broken in Northern Europe, had as its foundations nascent representative and democratic political institutions; an economy that was entrepreneurial, commercial, and capitalistic; middle classness; greater pluralism in the religious sphere; and a more inductive and scientific system of law and education. These differences mark the contrasts between the Middle Ages and modernity.

Spanish and Portuguese colonialism, and the institutions that went with them, lasted for over three hundred years, with little change. When independence finally came for most of the Latin American

Table 7.2 Founding contrasts between the United States and Latin America

	Latin America	*United States*
Dates	1492–1570	1620–1700
Economic	Mercantilist, statist	Capitalist, entrepreneurialist
Social	Feudal, two-class	Middle class and caste-based
Religious	Catholic, orthodox	Protestant, pluralist
Intellectual	Scholastic, deductive	Scientific, rationalist
Legal	Code law	Common law
Political	Absolutist, top-down	Democratic, participatory

countries in the 1820s, it was unaccompanied by any kind of social or political revolution as in the North American colonies. Instead, Latin America maintained its conservative, quasi-feudal past through most of the nineteenth century and on into the early twentieth. It was only with the global depression of the 1930s, accompanied by social and political collapse in almost every country, that Latin America began to change and modernize. During this entire period—three hundred years of colonialism and one hundred-plus years of independence, Latin America remained isolated from the main currents of modern international life.

There were seven main components in this change to modernity, which began in the 1930s. The first was cultural, a change in political values: Latin America became less fatalistic and more entrepreneurial and in charge of its own future. The second was economic: a shift from rural feudalism to urban capitalism and industrialization. Third, social change followed: a new middle class, urban trade unions, an organized peasantry, and new currents in the historic holders of power, the Church and the Army. Fourth, in religion: the Catholic Church modernized, while at the same time new Protestant and other groups appeared. Politically, fifth, the countries became more democratic and pluralistic. Sixth, the education system was improved and literacy increased. Finally, at the international level, Latin America's historic isolation broke down and the area became more integrated into global ideas and international affairs.

Latin America is, therefore, different from other developing areas. First, these are not "new nations" like those of South and Southeast Asia, the Middle East, Africa, and the British Caribbean that became independent after World War II; instead, Latin America has a long, five- hundred-year history behind it and, by now, 180-plus years of independence. Second, Latin America is not nearly so poor and underdeveloped as some parts of Asia, the Middle East, and Sub-Saharan Africa; rather, quite a number of countries in the area—Argentina, Brazil, Chile, Mexico, Uruguay, Venezuela—have broken out of Third World status and reached middle-income levels. Third, Latin America shares the Western hemisphere and lies right on the border of the United States. For all these reasons, Latin America needs to be treated differently than other developing areas.

There is still abundant poverty in Latin America (20–30 percent of the population, varying by countries) as well as vast income disparities (the widest in the world) between the rich and the poor. However, the percentage of people in poverty is way down from 50–60 percent twenty or thirty years ago, and several countries of the area have become predominantly (over 50 percent) middle class. They have also become over 70 percent urban, over 70 percent literate, and with a life expectancy not all that much lower than the United States. And, contrary to many popular notions, *New Yorker* cartoons, and *opera buffet* movies about the area, Latin America is no longer governed by comic-opera-men-on-horseback; instead, nineteen of the twenty countries (all except Cuba) are democratic.

The modernization, development, and democratization of Latin America change the givens of the situation and U.S. relations with the area. These *facts* have not been adequately recognized by U.S. policymakers who having rarely, if ever, visited the area are still influenced by the old (underdeveloped, incapable, comic-opera) stereotypes. But the reality is that, with the exception of Haiti, Nicaragua, and Bolivia, most of the Latin American countries have shown remarkable progress over the decades. They are not "basket cases" or "failed states" but rapidly developing and more modern countries. They should no longer be treated patronizingly and condescendingly, as the United States was long prone to do, as "little children" requiring our tutelage and guidance. Rather, they are increasingly mature nations that need to be approached with the assumptions of joint partnership and mutually beneficial relations. The days of referring to Latin America as "our little black and brown brothers" are, or should be, over.

The Asian cases that we've looked at earlier (South Korea, Taiwan, Singapore, India, now Malaysia, China, and maybe others), as well as those now of Latin America, suggest that when countries begin to develop and mature, the United States needs to change the nature of its relations with them. We can no longer treat them as poor, backward, "basket cases," and the recipients of U.S. foreign aid; but as developing, maturing partners that need to be treated with dignity, respect, and as equals. The older attitudes of U.S. "superiority" and other countries' inferiority will no longer do. Of course, if we wish our policies to succeed, we need to treat all countries with dignity and respect; but at the level of the countries we're talking about here, an extra measure is called for: true partnership.

U.S. Interests and Policy

U.S. relations with Latin America have *never* been put on the mature, normal basis that is clearly called for and that is characteristic of our relations with the developed countries of Western Europe or Japan. U.S. policy seems to alternate between benign neglect, which is often not so benign, and armed interventions, which do severe damage to the countries intervened as well as to our relations with the entire area. Essentially, the United States has always treated Latin America with indifference, taken it for granted, and dealt with it out of ignorance and condescension.

The strategic term used to describe our relations with Latin America, the counterpart to benign neglect, is "economy of force." Economy of force means that when the main threat is perceived to lie elsewhere— Germany in World War I, Germany and Japan in World War II, the Soviet Union during the Cold War, and now the fear of Middle Eastern terrorism—you need to devote all your energy and resources to that area. Therefore, you want to devote a minimum ("economy") of attention and resources to other areas—like Latin America. Hence, only the barest amount of diplomacy is given to Latin America while you concentrate on these other, presumably more important areas. As we see in the next chapter, these comments about benign neglect and economy of force apply even more so in sub-Saharan Africa.

The basic issue here is the asymmetry of wealth and power between the United States and Latin America. The United States is a big, rich, powerful nation—a superpower, presently the globe's only superpower. Most of the Latin American countries are small, poor, and weak. And the sad fact of life historically is that big, rich superpowers tend to take advantage of small, poor, weak nations. Latin America uses more colorful metaphors to describe these relations, referring to the United States as "the shark" and the Latin American countries as "the sardines." Of course, it is the big fish that eats or takes advantage of the smaller ones. But recently, as we've been arguing here, the "sardines" have become more prosperous and assertive; the old U.S. condescension and one-way policies will no longer work.

If you're a small country like those in Latin America, you're always going to be at a disadvantage in facing up to the neighborhood superpower. But the Latin American countries are not without their own resources, sometimes limited though they are, in countering U.S. influence and interventions. Among the techniques used are:

1. Appealing for the unity and solidarity among all the Latin American countries to counter U.S. power.
2. Banding together in agencies such as the Organization of American States (OAS).
3. Appealing to international law against U.S. interventions.
4. Appealing to world public opinion.
5. Seeking to divide public opinion and policymakers in the United States itself.

These strategies do not always prevent U.S. interventions, but they do serve often to lessen and shorten them and make them less destructive.

What are U.S. interests in Latin America? Historically, our goals there have been quite limited, encompassing the following:

1. Stability. This is the sine qua non of U.S. policy: stability in Latin America that leaves us free to pursue our interests in other parts of the world. For a long time this meant support for the authoritarian and military dictatorships of the area.
2. Access to the resources and markets of the region.
3. No hostile foreign powers—Germany, the Soviet Union, now Islamic terrorists—in the region. That was the reason for the Monroe Doctrine of 1823 and of virtually every U.S. policy since then.

The policy consequences of these principles and assumptions on the part of the United States have been enormous. In the 1830s and 1840s we took 40 percent of Mexico's national territory and annexed it to the United States. In the Spanish American War of 1898 we took Puerto Rico as a colony and established a protectorate over Cuba. In 1902 we separated Panama from Colombia to build our canal there—and then kept to ourselves the most valuable part of Panama, the

Canal Zone. In 1954, in the modern period, we overthrew a leftist government in Guatemala; in 1961 we intervened in Cuba to try to oust Castro; in 1965 we sent twenty-five thousand troops to reverse a democratic revolution in the Dominican Republic; in 1973 we employed CIA machinations to oust a socialist government in Chile; in 1983 we sent military forces into the tiny island of Grenada to oust a Marxist government; and in 1991 we invaded Panama to evict drug-dealing President Manuel Noriega, and so on, ad nauseum. It is not a nice picture: the United States repeatedly beating up on its smaller neighbors to the south. Isn't this what bullies do? And all of this done with one or another, often feeble, national security rationalization.

For most of the years of U.S.-Latin American relations, and especially during the long Cold War, American policy followed what was known as the "lesser evil doctrine." The United States seemed to favor authoritarians who signified stability, the prime goal of American policy, over democrats who were often unstable. More specifically, given the choice between a stable authoritarian who was anticommunist and sided with the United States on foreign policy, and a wobbly democrat who allowed free speech even for communists and flirted with nonalignment in the Cold War, the United States almost always chose ("the lesser evil") the anticommunist authoritarian. Naturally, that stand did not endear us to democrats, human rights advocates, and progressive reformers throughout Latin America.

The Castroite revolution in Cuba in the 1950s changed the givens of the U.S. calculus. For in the Cuban case we had a bloody dictator, Fulgencio Batista, who, instead of maintaining stability and an anticommunist stance, by his brutality and human rights violations made the conditions ripe for instability and a communist revolution to triumph.

The Cuban case forced a rethinking of U.S. policy under President John F. Kennedy. The goals of U.S. policy were still the same, stability and anticommunism; but now the means changed to the support of liberal democracy and economic development in Latin America as the best way to achieve stability. Support for dictators was out; support for democrats and development was in. Unfortunately, the Kennedy interregnum did not last; administrations changed; and the Cold War heated up again in the 1960s and 1970s. The United States reverted to its old and short-sighted policy of supporting dictators and military authoritarians—what some called "friendly tyrants."

Now it's harder, though not impossible, to do all these things in, or to, Latin America. For one thing, the Cold War is over; presently, the justification would have to be the war on terrorism, which seems far-fetched and unlikely to develop in the Latin American context. For another, international public opinion would be massively opposed to any further such U.S. military interventions. A third reason is that the United States has fewer resources and is preoccupied with Afghanistan, Iran, Iraq, North Korea, and Pakistan; it is not prepared to contemplate another large U.S. military operation in the Latin American part of the world. And fourth, the Latin American countries themselves are now more developed, more mature, and assertive; except in extreme circumstances, it makes no sense anymore for the United States to even contemplate military action in Latin America.

Logically, therefore, we are back where the discussion began: on the need for a stable, mature policy that treats Latin America as partners instead of immature children, that builds partnerships rather than condescends. Latin America has developed and progressed enormously over the last half century; these are no longer, contrary to some still existing popular stereotypes, "banana republics." Instead, they are complex, developing, increasingly stable, and mature nations. And with their own interests to advance *alongside* those of the United States.

The other imperative that makes this new relationship so necessary is our increased *inter*dependence with Latin America. On a host of issues both of us require each other's cooperation. Think of the wide variety of issues on which we and Latin America are independent and how different these are from the short list of U.S. interests enumerated earlier: oil imports, natural gas, trade, investment, democracy, human rights, immigration, labor supplies, water resources, acid rain, pollution, the environment, conservation, drugs, tourism, air flights, shipping, counterterrorism, debt and banking, manufacturing, crime, health and health care. Note that virtually every one of these is an international issue and not just a domestic one, or what political scientists call "inter-mestic," a complex mixture of international and domestic features. It is unlikely, therefore, that any of them can be solved by unilateral U.S. action alone. We are in a position, unlike in the past, where we need Latin America and its cooperation as much as they need us. That is what makes us interdependent and *forces* us to formulate a new basis for U.S. policy in the region.

Problems and Issues

After two decades, the 1960s and 1970s, of Cold War-dictated support for authoritarian regimes in Latin America, U.S. policy began to change in the 1980s and 1990s. The Kennedy era idea was revived that, in the long run, support for democracy and human rights was better for U.S. policy than close association with military authoritarians who abused human rights. Several other factors were occurring during this time that contributed to the shift of policy: the Cold War was winding down and the Communist threat lessened; the authoritarian regimes were discredited in their own countries; and, starting with Jimmy Carter and expanding under Ronald Reagan and George H. W. Bush, the democracy/human rights movement was growing in the United States. The collapse of communism in 1989–1991 in the Soviet Union and Eastern Europe gave rise to a sense of euphoria that the United States had the correct economic formula as well as the right political one that it could export to Latin America.

With communism collapsing and authoritarianism discredited, democracy and free markets by the 1990s appeared to be "the only games in town." A new policy, called "The Washington Consensus," reminiscent of Kennedy's "Alliance for Progress," was formulated by the United States, which had at its base three legs:

1. Support for democracy and human rights as the best basis for long-term stability.
2. Support for free markets, which carried with it the need to privatize and reform the Latin American economies, including balanced budgets, austerity, and state-downsizing.
3. Support for free trade, which called for the end of protectionism in both the United States and Latin America.

Since the early 1990s, this has basically been the policy, not only in Latin America but toward other world areas as well.

However, as we all know, three-legged stools are inherently unstable. First, democracy in Latin America is still often wobbly, not well institutionalized or consolidated—illiberal rather than full democracy. Second, because of its long mercantilist tradition, capitalism in Latin America has not worked out very well either, with many countries returning to a more European-like statist model. Third, free trade, which most economists believe has a multiplier effect on economic growth (for every dollar invested, you get two in return), is being reversed—not by the Latin American countries that have opened their markets but by U.S. protectionism. The result in Latin America has been a new wave of populist regimes—Hugo Chávez in Venezuela, Evo Morales in Bolivia, Rafael Corea in Ecuador, Daniel Ortega in Nicaragua, and now Mauricio Funes in El Salvador—whose democratic credentials are suspect and whose economic policies may lead to ruin. So much for the Washington "Consensus."

Meanwhile, a number of new issues have come to the fore:

- Drugs have become a major element in U.S.-Latin American relations; in some countries, the narco-traffickers threaten to take over parts of the state.
- Immigration has become a hot issue across borders; sentiment is strong that there must be immigration reform.
- The war on terrorism has once again diverted U.S. attention from Latin America—except as there are small Arab Islamic communities in the area and as the terrorist threat has again focused policy on our porous southern border.
- Many Latin American countries are diversifying their trade away from the United States and toward Asia and Europe.
- China has become a major player in the area—so far limiting its involvement mainly to commercial issues.
- Quite a number of Latin American countries are following a more independent foreign policy no longer in accord with the United States—for example, on the wars in Afghanistan, Iraq, and on terrorism. The U.S. presumption of hegemony in the area may be over.
- The Latin American countries are joining together in international organizations that often exclude the United States, such as MERCOSUR, the South American common market or ALBA, the alliance of anti-American states led by Venezuela.

Most of these newer developments point toward a more independent (away from the United States) Latin America and a less-controlling, less-"hegemonic" United States.

Country-Specific Issues

We tend to treat Latin America as a whole, and indeed there are common histories and patterns among the countries. But the Latin American countries are also quite different from each other—and increasingly more so. We do not have the space here to analyze U.S. relations with all the individual countries,[1] but we do need to consider some of the more important ones.

Argentina

Argentina is a large (the size of the United States east of the Mississippi), wealthy (in natural resources), sophisticated (mainly European) country that has long thought of itself as a rival and counterweight to the United States on the South American continent. Its capital of Buenos Aires considers itself the "Paris of Latin America"; until the mid-1920s, Argentina had a per capita income level higher than that of the United States. But since then, Argentina has fallen precipitously to the point where its per capita income is only one-fourth the U.S. level; its social and political institutions have followed a similar downward trajectory. As a reflection of this downward turn and the Argentine preoccupation with its causes, Buenos Aires has more psychiatrists per capita than Manhattan! As my students like to say, it's a thoroughly "screwed up" country.

Argentina behaves totally irresponsibly on the international stage, refusing to pay its debts, printing ever-more worthless paper money, and periodically going belly-up financially. Not only has it fallen way behind the United States but now it has also fallen behind its archrival Brazil as the main power in South America. It remains a rich country agriculturally and in terms of natural resources, but its social, economic, and political institutions and capacities are severely retarded. Quite naturally, the nature of its fall and the reasons for it are *the* main preoccupations of the Argentines. Hence, Argentina is prickly, often difficult to deal with, intensely nationalistic, and angry that it has fallen so far. Still an important player because of its size and resources but not a major one, Argentina will likely remain a marginal country in global politics and in terms of U.S. relations with the area.

Brazil

Brazil has replaced Argentina as the dominant country in Latin America. It is, in contrast to Argentina, a rising power in South America and globally.

Brazil is the fourth largest country in the world in terms of land mass, comparable to Canada, China, and the United States, the fifth largest in population, and ninth in gross domestic product. Brazil has immense resources and has recently emerged as one of the world's largest agricultural producers. It has developed manufacturing, industry, and technology; recent offshore petroleum discoveries may vault Brazil into the ranks of the world's major powers.

Brazil has recently been included among the BRIC (*B*razil, *R*ussia, *I*ndia, *C*hina), countries that may in the next half-century crash the list of the world's top five (after the United States, China, and Japan) producing nations. Internally, Brazil is developing its highway system, its universities, and its infrastructure at a rapid rate. There is an old saying about Brazil that goes, "Brazil is the land of the future—and always will be." But now Brazil's development is so rapid that it seems likely to achieve its potential.

Diplomatically and politically, Brazil is also making great strides. It restored democracy in 1985 and now has had nearly twenty years of stable, effective government. It has emerged as a leader in MERCOSUR, the "Common Market of the South," on the South American continent. The United States recognizes Brazil as the dominant influence in South America. But Brazil has ambitions that go beyond regional power status; it is operating ambitiously on the world stage. Its diplomacy functions quietly but effectively in sub-Saharan Africa, in the Third World generally, and in Europe. Brazil, like India, is seeking a seat on the UN Security Council and believes its size and importance merit it a place among the world's great powers. It, therefore, behooves the United States to get closer to this rising power.

Colombia

Colombia is one of the most beautiful countries in the world and one of the most misunderstood. Its verdant vegetation, close to the equator, is so lush-green that it is almost blinding to the eye, matching the color of the emeralds that Colombia produces in abundance.

In the Western press, however, Colombia is best known for its less attractive features: as the home of some of the last Marxist guerilla movements to exist in all Latin America, as a worldwide center of drug production and trafficking, and the home of some truly mind-numbing political violence that has persisted over the decades.

But Colombia is much more than just drugs, violence, and guerillas. Not only is it a beautiful country, but it is also a large, important, and highly productive one. With over forty million people, Colombia is the fifth largest country in Latin America and with immense natural resources. It has oil, coal, abundant and rich farmland, and still largely untapped mineral resources. Long known as the world's main supplier of coffee, Colombia has by now diversified its economy and is, among other things, the largest supplier of flowers to the United States and European markets.

Long plagued by violence, Colombia under President Alvaro Uribe had recently begun to recover from that scourge. Uribe took important steps against the remaining guerilla groups, clamped down on narco-trafficking, and greatly reduced political violence. Colombia's cities, highways, and rural areas are now safer than in any recent era. The United States aligned itself closely with Uribe's efforts; but given Colombia's size and importance, the United States needs to sustain a long-term relationship with the country even after the issues-of-the-moment (drugs and guerillas) are resolved.

Mexico

Mexico may be the most important country in the *world*, from the point of view of U.S. foreign policy. That statement may seem surprising to some in that Mexico has no nuclear weapons and is not a military or strategic threat to the United States. But there is no country in the world, because of all those interdependence factors of which we spoke earlier—and especially immigration—that has more capacity to affect our domestic economy, society, and politics.

Mexico is now a country of 110 million persons. It is the second largest country (after Brazil) in Latin America. It has, like the other countries considered here, vast resources, including a large, skilled and unskilled labor supply and huge quantities of oil and natural gas. It is not well known that Mexico is our second-largest trading partner, behind only Canada but, surprising to many, ahead of both China and Japan. In addition, Mexico is no longer a poor country: with a per capita income of nearly $10,000 per year (comparable to Argentina, Chile, and Brazil), it has, like these others, a large middle-class eager to purchase U.S. products. And again, like the other countries analyzed here, Mexico is no longer just an agricultural and primary products-exporting country but a major manufacturing and industrializing one as well. Now, think of what it would mean security-wise if we could get a good share of our oil and natural gas via pipeline directly across the Rio Grande from Mexico instead of having to ship it halfway around the world from those potentially violent and unstable sheik-doms of the Middle East.

Mexico's greatest impact on the United States currently is through immigration. And through such other "interdependency factors" as pollution, drugs, disease, water supplies, crime, and so on. If we think that we presently have difficulties dealing with Mexican emigration to the United States, think of what a destabilized Mexico, either economically or politically, would do to our relations: it would immediately send *millions* of Mexicans across the border into the United States. And with enormous expense and mostly burdensome consequences at the local, county, state, and national levels.

The United States must, therefore, assist Mexico and come to its defense at all costs. The last thing we need is a destabilized Mexico right on our border. Or a Mexico of high joblessness, of a failed economy or political system, or a country where violent drug lords have taken over whole sectors of Mexican life, spilling their violence across the border into the United States. The United States, therefore, has a vital interest in maintaining a stable, happy, economically prosperous, and democratic Mexico. The stakes in Mexico are as high or higher as with any country anywhere in the world.

Venezuela

Venezuela had long been one of the richest, best-educated, most middle-class, most urban, and most democratic of all the Latin American countries. It almost literally (like Kuwait or Saudi Arabia) floats on oil and has other vast resources as well—agricultural, mineral, water, everything. For forty years from 1959 to 1999 Venezuela had been a model of stability and democracy.

But trouble was brewing just below the surface. The benefits from oil revenues had been very unevenly distributed, creating a large, urban middle-class but leaving over half the population mired in poverty. Though democratic, the political system was very corrupt and patronage-dominated. Although early efforts had been made to "sew the petroleum" (use oil revenues to diversify the economy), by the 1980s petroleum sales constituted 80 percent of export revenues, at a time of falling prices. In addition, like other "petro-states," many Venezuelans had turned complacent and even lazy, reasoning that, since the country was so rich, they need not bother to work anymore. Oil wealth similarly gave rise to the popular notion that, if the country was so rich but the wealth was not trickling down to the people, it must be the fault of corrupt politicians and "the system."

In this setting, along came charismatic, nationalistic, socialist, anti-American president Hugo Chávez. Chávez was elected (and reelected) democratically, but he has governed in a way that has largely destroyed Venezuela's democratic institutions—congress, judiciary, political parties, independent media, universities, interest groups, and civil society. He has also, in his efforts to help the poor, severely damaged the economy, wiped out the middle class, and made Venezuela into even more of a "one-crop" (oil) economy than it was before. Chávez is a throwback to the nineteenth-century tradition of one-man, *caudillo* (but a socialist *caudillo*) man-on-horseback politics that is no longer appropriate in a modernizing, complex country like Venezuela.

As long as he confines his "twenty-first-century socialism" to Venezuela, meanwhile continuing to sell us oil, Chávez's domestic policies should be of little concern to the United States. But Chávez has threatened to cut the United States off from his oil, renationalized the oil industry, and taken steps in support of the guerillas in next-door Colombia. He has also invited the Russians to use Venezuela as a base for military operations, allied himself with communist dictator Fidel Castro, and aided the rise of like-minded Marxist-populists in Bolivia, Ecuador, El Salvador, Nicaragua, and Paraguay.

Venezuela is not a military threat to the United States, but it is a cause of trouble throughout the hemisphere. And with its size, resources, oil wealth, and meddling in other countries, it is much too important for the United States to ignore.

Conclusion

Most Americans, including most U.S. policymakers, will be surprised by the analysis in this chapter. For most Americans still harbor a prejudiced and, by now, very wrong and outdated image of Latin America as comical, undeveloped, unstable, unserious, unsuccessful, and, therefore, unworthy of U.S. attention or the commitment of strategic resources.

But as we have seen here, that is an old-fashioned and mistaken view. Almost all the countries of Latin America have been developing rapidly over the last half century. Quite a number of them have "taken off" economically, become predominantly middle class, and achieved (especially those countries highlighted here, and also Chile, Costa Rica, and Uruguay) what the World Bank calls "upper middle income" status. With their size, populations, resources, and markets, all these countries have become important to U.S. interests. Moreover, sharing this geography called the Western hemisphere, and increasingly interdependent with the United States, they are natural partners with, and natural markets for, the United States. Among the countries, all of them are newly important to the United States but Brazil and Mexico stand out as most important.

Yet U.S. policy toward the area has long been, and remains sporadic, inconsistent, often schizophrenic, and characterized by long periods of neglect (benign or otherwise) interspersed with dramatic interventions. But in a context of rapid development and modernization in Latin America, this will no longer do, especially if one bears in mind increasing anti-Americanism and hostility to the United States in other parts of the world.

The United States needs to put its relations with Latin America on the same regular, normal basis that we have long maintained with Western Europe and Japan. Given Latin America's rising importance, its resources, its swelling middle class and markets, and its Western orientation and location within our hemisphere, we need to accord it far more importance than we have hitherto. We need to elevate Latin America several notches up in our rank-ordering of regional priorities—certainly to a level equal to that of Eastern Europe, Russia, South Asia, and maybe even the Middle East.

In addition, in this now globalized world, we have become mutually interdependent with Latin America in all kinds of complex ways—social, economic, cultural, political, strategic. Therefore, we need to pay more and serious attention to Latin America, stop treating it as if it were a bunch of banana republics, and commence a true partnership with the region that has been lacking in the past.

Note

1. For a country-by-country analysis, see Howard J. Wiarda and Harvey F. Kline (eds.), *Latin American Politics and Development* (Boulder, CO: Westview Press, 7th ed., 2010).

Suggested Readings

Atkins, G. Pope. *Latin America and the Caribbean in the International System* (Boulder, CO: Westview Press, 1999).

Dearly, Glen. *The Latin Americans* (Boulder, CO: Westview, 1983).

———. *The Public Man: An Interpretation of Latin America and other Catholic Countries* (Amherst, MA: University of Massachusetts Press, 1977).

Hamilton, Bernice. *Political Thought in Sixteenth Century Spain* (Oxford, UK: Oxford University Press, 1963).

Kryzanek, Michael. *U.S.-Latin American Relations* (New York: Praeger, 1992).

Langley, Lester. *The Americas in the Modern Age* (New Haven: Yale University Press, 2005).

Morse, Richard. *New World Surroundings: Culture and Ideology in the Americas* (Baltimore: John Hopkins University Press, 1989).

Van Cott, Donne Lee. *Indigenous Peoples and Democracy in Latin America* (New York: St. Martin's, 1994).

Veliz, Claudio. *The Centralist Tradition in Latin America* (Princeton, NJ: Princeton University Press, 1980).

Wiarda, Howard J. *The Democratic Revolution in Latin America* (New York: Holmes and Meier, 1992).

———. *Latin American Politics: A New World of Possibility* (Belmont, CA: Woodsworth, 1995).

Wiarda, Howard J. and Harvey Kline (eds.). *Latin American Politics and Development* (Boulder, CO: Westview Press, 2010).

CHAPTER 8

Africa

The image most of us carry around in our heads of Africa, largely shaped by television coverage, is of starving, often dying children, with bloated bellies, covered with flies. Or perhaps it is of Darfur and its poor, emaciated, brutalized people; or of the genocide in Rwanda, as pictured in the movie "Hotel Rwanda." Or maybe the images we have are of the AIDS epidemic in Africa and the terrible and widespread death it has inflicted. Or perhaps of thieving white businessmen and politicians, ripping off the continent's natural wealth as in "Black Diamonds," or holding back black majority rule as in South Africa.

These images are not entirely wrong, as we see in more detail in this chapter. They are propagated by the media of movies and television, which tend to emphasize—because that is seen as "good television"—the most vivid, most dramatic, most blood-curdling scenes. If we only watched television or went to the movies, we would think that the only things that happened in Africa were civil wars, violence, bloodshed, AIDS, and mass starvation. Those elements *are* part of the truth of Africa, but they are not the whole truth. Lots of other things are going on in Africa.

Actually, in the last fifteen years, Africa has not been doing altogether badly. The high point of the violence, AIDS, and civil wars in Africa, which shaped our image of the area, was the early-to-mid 1990s. But much has changed since then. There have been many elections; the number of democratic states is on the rise. Quite a number of African countries have seen a significant rise in their per capita incomes. Foreign investment, led by the Chinese but also including Brazil, India, and other up-and-coming states, is pouring in, mainly to exploit Africa's considerable resources but also adding to jobs and income levels within Africa. And, of course, if China is interested in Africa, whom many security analysts see as our next, great, twenty-first-century superpower rival, then the United States has to be interested in Africa as well. That, in part, lies behind the State Department's recent renewed interest in Africa and the Defense Department's recent creation of a new and important regional command for Africa, AFRICOM. We will have more to say about the U.S. role in Africa later in the chapter.

We should not exaggerate these accomplishments. Africa remains very poor, the poorest continent. The number of genuine democracies is still very small, about 20 percent of the countries. Hunger, malnutrition, and AIDS and other diseases still devastate the population. Corruption is widespread. Often the government and its bureaucracy, woefully inept and underinstitutionalized, do not function as a moderately competent and honest government should. There is a lack of infrastructure—farm-to-market roads, port facilities, highways, bridges, and so on—and civil society is weak. Violence, civil war, slaughter, and rape as an instrument of war or genocide still stalk the countryside. In the cities, drugs, crime, gangs, and ethnic or tribal violence are endemic. Life expectancy is short; quality of life, low; and the value often placed on life itself, cheap. The problems continue to multiply.

And yet, even with all these problems, which we should by no means minimize, Africa is changing. The continent is undoubtedly better off than it was fifty years ago when all of these "new nations" burst onto the world scene after decades and even centuries of colonialism. If we look at the per capita income figures for those years, most of the countries fell into the $100–300 range. Now, as we see in detail in the next section, *no* country is in that low range. They have *all* raised their standard of living considerably. That does not mean they have suddenly become affluent countries; quite the contrary. But they are not hopeless either.

A decade-and-a-half ago I wrote that the situation in many African states, and in the continent as a whole, was chaotic. And that meant, in a foreign policy sense, that the United States should not pay serious attention to the area, outside of an occasional humanitarian intervention. Today, Africa's condition has changed sufficiently that I would no longer say either of those two things. Africa's condition is not hopeless, and we should be paying serious attention to the area.

Socioeconomic Background

Of the forty-eight countries in sub-Saharan Africa,[1] thirty-two or two-thirds of them are ranked as low-income countries (LICs; see table 8.1), which means they are among the world's poorest countries. Latin America, Southeast Asia, and the Middle East also contain some poor countries, but none of these contain as many poor countries as does Africa. In these other developing areas, poor countries are becoming the exception; but in Africa poverty is still the way of life of a majority of the countries and people. No other continent or world region has as many poor people and poor countries as does Africa.

There is not a single developed or high-income country in all of Africa. That makes it difficult for the United States to have good or extensive business, commerce, or trade relations with very many of the African countries—or very many relations of any kind. Of the forty-eight African countries, only six are ranked as upper-middle-income countries (UMCs). UMCs are defined as countries having per capita income of between $3,706 and $11,455 on a yearly basis. The group includes Botswana, Gabon, Mauritius, Mayotte, Seychelles, and South Africa. These are the only countries that are truly "making it" to developed-country status. And yet even then there are questions, because five of the six exist in special circumstances: South Africa (discussed in more detail later) is almost as much a European country as it is African; Botswana is wealthier because it has diamonds and benefits from neighboring South Africa's wealth; Mauritius, Mayotte, and the Seychelles are all island nations off the African coast that benefit from special trade or neocolonial relations with the former metropole. That leaves Gabon as the only upper-middle-income country to have truly made it on its own. But Gabon, though comparatively wealthy, should not be thought of as the poster-child for Africa: it has abundant oil and timber, which account for its wealth, but it is also corrupt and only weakly institutionalized.

Table 8.1 African per capita income

Country	Per capita income (in $)	Category
Argola	4,400	LMC
Benin	1,310	LIC
Botswana	12,420	UMC
Burkina Faso	1,120	LIC
Burundi	330	LIC
Cameroon	2,120	LMC
Cape Verde	2,940	LMC
Central African Republic	740	LIC
Chad	1,280	LIC
Comoros		
Congo Democratic Republic	290	LIC
Congo Republic	2,750	LMC
Côte d'Ivoire	1,590	LIC
Equatorial Guinea	520	LIC
Ethiopia	780	LIC
Gabon	13,080	UMC
Gambia, The	1,140	LIC
Ghana	1,330	LIC
Guinea	1,120	LIC
Guinea-Bissau	470	LIC
Kenya	1,540	LIC
Lesotho	1,890	LMC
Liberia	290	LIC
Madagascar	920	LIC
Malawi	750	LIC
Mali	1,040	LIC
Mauritania	2,120	LIC
Mauritius	11,390	UMC
Mayotte	UMC	
Mozambique	690	LIC
Namibia	5,120	LMC
Niger	630	LIC
Nigeria	1,770	LIC
Rwanda	860	LIC
Sao Tomé and Principe	–	LIC
Senegal	1,640	LIC
Seychelles	15,450	UMC
Sierra Leone	660	LIC
Somalia	–	LIC
South Africa	9,560	UMC

Table 8.1 Continued

Country	Per capita income (in $)	Category
Sudan	1,880	LMC
Swaziland	4,930	LMC
Tanzania	1,200	LIC
Togo	800	LIC
Uganda	920	LIC
Zambia	1,220	LIC
Zimbabwe		LIC

UMC: Upper middle income country; LIC: Low-income country.

Another group of countries is called "lower-middle-income countries (LMCs)" by the World Bank. These are countries that are not so poor as the LICs and not yet making it as are the UMCs. The list of LMCs includes eight countries: Angola, Cameroon, Cape Verde, the Republic of the Congo, Lesotho, Sudan, and Swaziland. But here again we have to add some qualifiers: Lesotho and Swaziland benefit from the run-off effect of South Africa's wealth, while Angola, Cameroon, Cape Verde, and the Sudan have oil or other precious export items.

That means a total of only fourteen—less than a third—of Africa's forty-eight countries have even *begun* the process of development; and of these fourteen only a handful are making it on their own through indigenous efforts. The rest either benefit from nearby wealth in other countries or have such rich resources—oil or diamonds—that they can hardly miss. Meanwhile, there are those other thirty-two still mired in extreme poverty. If you combine the LICs (thirty-two) with the countries whose main claim to fame is someone else's wealth or so many natural resources that you can't miss, the number of countries doing well on their own is very limited—less than half a dozen. The prospects for the other forty-plus, therefore, do not look so good.

It should be understood that, when we speak of LICs or poor countries in Africa, we are talking about real poverty, what Paul Collier recently called "The Bottom Billion." This is poverty that is mind-numbing and is likely to send a first-time visitor into culture shock: the dirt, the flies, the disease, the malnutrition, the bloated bellies of the children (not from too much food but too little), the malnutrition-related diseases, the malformed people (no medical care) or those with missing limbs, AIDS, starvation, the sheer misery and desperation of it all. What can be done? Can *anything* be done?

Actually, the situation in Africa is not quite as bleak as portrayed here. There was a time, only forty years ago, when the World Bank numbers showed the yearly income of most Africans as under $300. That means under one dollar a day per person. And even that low number took no account of the *distribution* of income. For the fact was, even in this early time, most of the wealth was concentrated in very few hands. The bulk of the population had *no* income, indeed existed at a very low level on the basis of trade and barter and was, in effect, completely outside of a modern, money market economy.

Much of that has changed now. Look again at the numbers in table 8.1. *No* country is any longer in the $300 per person per year range. Twenty-seven of the forty-eight countries are above the $1,000 figure. Several are in the $2,000–4,000 range and six are up near $10,000 or above. Even the poorest countries have moved up in the rankings and are closing on the $1,000 threshold. We should not glorify these numbers or cite them as a way of helping us ignore the truly horrendous poverty and disease that still exist. But it is also possible to read these numbers, as suggested in our introduction, and see that the situation in Africa is not entirely hopeless. Indeed, there is substantial reason for greater optimism.

Given all this poverty, disease, and even helplessness, the arguments for ignoring Africa are powerful. It sometimes seems so hopeless and we have relatively few interests there, and even fewer vital or security interests. We could easily say that we have no major interests there and let it go at that. But we do have interests—a moral interest in relieving poverty and disease, even if we do not benefit directly from that. We also have an interest in advancing democracy and human rights in Africa. Certainly, African-Americans, including the president, have an interest in their roots in Africa and in seeing that Africa does well. And now, with China, India, and other global competitors buying up Africa's abundant resources (oil, precious metals, diamonds, timber) and newfound threats of potential terrorism emerging out of some of Africa's failed states, we do have some vital strategic interests there. That was behind a recent step-up in U.S. diplomacy in Africa and the creation of a regional military command, AFRICOM, for Africa. But the question remains: what exactly should U.S. policy be toward this continent that we have never paid much serious attention to before?

Historical Background

Why is it that Africa is so poor? Why are there no developed or fully First World countries there? What holds Africa back? What is Africa's problem? Why does it lag behind—often far behind—other developing areas in Asia, Latin America, and the Middle East? What priority should the United States accord the continent?

Providing answers to these questions is a tricky business. For one thing, the issue is tied up in American domestic politics, as more and more African-Americans are becoming interested in their African roots and the fate of the countries there. For another, the issue is especially sensitive, often involving stereotypes ("All Africans are this or that") and, therefore, the charge, real or imagined, of racism. If you're a Marxist, it's easy to blame Africa's troubles on colonialism and imperialism; more recent Marxist scholars of Africa have taken to blaming the World Bank or the International Monetary Fund (IMF). Non-Marxists who focus on African political culture or the indigenous, as distinct from international, origins of Africa's problems similarly run the risk of having their careers destroyed by the racism charge. The issue is: do we blame the Africans themselves for their own ills, or does the cause lie further back in some combination of outside forces and influences?

We begin with the early history. First, there is much evidence that the earliest humans evolved in Africa and from there spread out to other regions and continents. In terms of human history, Africa claims primacy. Second, in the premodern era there is much evidence of advanced cultures and civilizations in Africa, which remain largely unknown to us because they were isolated and, therefore, unknown in the dominant European culture and historiography. Would or could these societies have evolved into more modern societies if left to their own devices and historical development? The answer is: we don't know because along came European colonialism and imperialism, which for centuries interrupted and frustrated the natural course of African development.

Colonialism, imperialism, and the African slave trade, which went hand-in-hand with the other two, began as early as the fifteenth century. In West Africa the Portuguese were the first slave traders, but do not forget that, in East Africa, Indian as well as Middle Eastern merchants and slavers had been plying the trade for centuries. And do not let us ignore that in this nefarious trade African kings and tribal leaders were as guilty as everyone else, supplying the slaves to the outsiders who then shipped them to the rest of the world. Eventually, almost everyone was involved: Portugal, Spain, France, Great Britain, the Netherlands, Belgium, Germany, China, India, and the Middle East.

Colonialism and imperialism were unmitigated evils wherever they were practiced, but some forms were more evil than others. What colonialism did was to destroy the ancient African cultures and civilizations noted earlier, drain the continent of its resources and manpower, which were then used for the benefit of the colonial countries and not the colonies, and distort—perhaps forever—the developmental potential of the future African states. Colonialism also imposed artificial boundaries on Africa that had nothing to do with African realities and left a situation of meaningless borders in terms of the geographic and ethnic realities that carried over to the national period, tribal and ethnic groups divided by these boundaries, and in other cases tribes brought together within these borders that had nothing to do with each other. Among the colonial powers, Belgium is usually thought of as the cruelest and most oppressive, but the others were not far behind.

The slave trade lasted, with some variation among countries, through approximately the mid-nineteenth century, when both the trade and slavery itself began to be abolished—including in the United States. However, colonialism and imperialism continued in most areas of Africa for another hundred years. This means that, in some parts of Africa, colonialism and imperialism had been practiced for four or five hundred years. That half-millennium of exploitation meant that Africa was systematically stripped and robbed of its immense natural resources; its most ambitious and energetic people were shipped off to other continents in the slave trade; and Africa had no opportunity to develop in its own way or with its own culture. Colonialism and imperialism also gave rise to the notions that Africa "was not up to it," that its people were lazy and stupid, and that it was incapable of governing itself without European or, eventually, American guidance, paternally delivered.

Colonialism was so pervasive and lasted so long that over time it gave rise to what have been called "white tribes" within the "Dark Continent." In places like Kenya (British), Zimbabwe (British—formerly Southern Rhodesia), Angola (Portuguese), Mozambique (Portuguese), and South Africa (Dutch), the Europeans had been there so long, often hundreds of years, that they considered themselves part of Africa. They often had built the infrastructure, developed the farms, and founded the industries that had enabled some parts of Africa to begin an economic take-off in the early-to-mid-twentieth century.

When colonialism or, in the South African case, *apartheid* abruptly ended, the white tribes were faced with a dilemma. They had often built their countries but they were no longer welcome in Africa; on the other hand, they had lived outside of their native countries for so long that they were no longer comfortable or welcome back there either. Teresa Heinz Kerry (Senator John Kerry's wife) is from one of these families, having grown up in Mozambique and with a long Portuguese family history there, only to be driven out of the country at great costs to her family as well as her former country, and forced to find a new life elsewhere.

Colonialism and imperialism finally came to an end after World War II, in the mid-twentieth century. It came to an end for a variety of reasons: after the war the colonial countries lacked the resources to maintain their empires; there was international pressure to grant independence to their colonies; the colonials no longer had the stomach for it; and within the colonies, guerrilla and terrorist liberation movements were attacking the colonial forces. The number of independent African states began to swell in the 1950s; by 1958–1960 a *host* of new African states had achieved independence and joined the United Nations.

From the beginning, these new nations were beset by a large number of insurmountable problems. Most of them wrote new and democratic constitutions; they also tended to hold up one or another form of socialism as the ideal to strive for. But they also lacked political parties, efficient bureaucracies, investment for development, critical infrastructure, governments that worked and delivered real social and economic programs, and entrepreneurs that could produce jobs and stimulate development. Meanwhile, there were often civil wars between the tribes and ethnicities that made up the society, uprisings by dissident tribes, border disputes to settle because the new *national* borders following the old colonial divisions made no sense, and virtually constant meddling by the old and new (U.S., USSR) colonial powers.

By the mid-to-late 1960s, almost all the new African countries were in trouble. Many of the new democracies had surrendered to military-authoritarian rule. But the armed forces in Africa were often as disorganized and unprofessional as the rest of society. The new military leaders were generally corrupt, violated human and civil rights, and oppressed their own peoples. Although some still tried, it was no longer possible to blame all of Africa's troubles on colonialism and imperialism. By this time, the 1970s and 1980s, Africa was as much responsible for its underdevelopment and lack of progress as were the mysterious "outside powers" who are still often blamed.

The 1980s and 1990s were a period of great upheaval in Africa. There were wars, revolutions, violence, AIDS, uprisings, conflict, natural disasters, genocides, and almost endemic strife. Some countries, even during this violent period, managed to make a transition back to democracy and to stimulate development. A few even "took off"—the handful of success stories in Africa. The early 1990s may have been the high point of civil war and violence in Africa.

Since then, things have begun to change, at least in some countries. Democracy is spreading; successful elections have been held; violence and genocide have been diminished, in part because of the presence of international peacekeepers; and capital is now pouring in. New investments, by China, India, the EU, and the United States, are stimulating the growth of jobs and local economies even as they continue to drain Africa of its natural resources.

So has Africa at long last settled down? Is it now poised to embark on a new era of democracy and development? Can it resolve its long-standing problems and issues and begin to take its place among the family of developed nations? It is probably too soon to be that enthusiastic. Africa has a very long way to go. It is likely that, at least in the immediate future, we will see as much chaos as progress.

The United States has never given much consideration to Africa. First, except for Cold War issues, the United States has never thought that Africa was worth paying much attention to—although one could not say that publicly because of domestic political reasons. So except for the Cold War-related conflicts in the Congo in the 1960s, Angola and Mozambique in the 1970s, and South Africa and the Horn of Africa in the 1980s, the United States has generally practiced benign neglect toward Africa—even more so than our neglect of Latin America. Second, the United States has generally felt that, as the main former colonial powers who, therefore, knew Africa better than we did, the European countries should have primary responsibility for "policing" and peacekeeping in Africa, just as we "policed" in our sphere of influence, the Caribbean, Mexico, and Central and South America.

But now, the United States is expanding and diversifying its interests in the area. In part, this is driven by a recognition of Africa's rising importance, in part by Europe's unwillingness or failure to adequately assist or police the area, and in part by rising competition for Africa's resources by China and others. American interest in the area is also influenced by rising African-American concerns about the countries of their origins, in particular President Barack Obama's interest in his own African parentage, and by the fact the United States, still seen as the world's fireman, policeman, and all-around savior, gets blamed for not rescuing Africa from its own genocides, civil wars, and violence. We often get sucked into African disputes whether or not we have any vital national interest in getting involved.

Ironically, it was President George W. Bush, usually derided because of Iraq as a terrible foreign policy president, who began America's reengagement with Africa. Bush provided more financial assistance to the fight against AIDS than any previous American president; he increased foreign aid to Africa through the innovative Millennium Challenge Account; and he authorized the creation of AFRICOM, the first time the Defense Department had created a central command specifically for Africa and aimed at facilitating peacekeeping, democracy promotion, and humanitarian intervention. Bush's policies were flawed, but at least they represented a start; we will have to see if his successors continue these policies or modify them in various ways.

Meanwhile, what should be U.S. policy toward Africa?[2]

- Stand strongly for democracy and human rights even while recognizing we cannot create democracy overnight in the world's poorest nations.
- Assist Africa at grassroots levels with literacy programs, education, health care, and civil society-building.
- Combat corruption and work on good-government/accountability issues.
- Increase U.S. diplomatic capacities throughout the continent.
- Help develop Africa's rich agricultural, mining, energy, and forestry potential; encourage U.S. investment.
- Forge a new multilateral diplomacy in Africa so it is not always the United States alone that must respond to every ringing of the fire bell.
- Help Africa develop its own ability to do peacekeeping, conflict resolution, and nation-building.
- Emphasize Africa's *importance* to the United States and, as in Latin America, portray this as an *opportunity-based* foreign policy objective and not just, as in the past, as threat-based.

Country Cases

South Africa

South Africa has, by far, the largest economy in Africa and is among the top twenty-five largest economies in the world. Its per capita income of $9,560 is also at or among the highest in Africa, though only at about one-fourth the level of the wealthy West European countries. Though well-off by African standards, South Africa's wealth is terribly unevenly distributed, largely following racial lines. White South Africans tend to be upper and middle class and try to maintain a European life style, while black South Africans—although there is now a small but rising black middle class—tend to be lower class, impoverished, and at about the same level as the rest of Africa.

South Africa has an unusual history, culture, and sociology that make it different from the other African states. The colony at the Cape of Good Hope (Cape Town), the southern tip of Africa, was founded by Dutch sailors in 1651 as part of the European (Portuguese, Spanish, Dutch, French, British) effort to expand their Asian trade and colonies by going around Africa. Finding relatively few indigenous Africans in the Cape, the Dutch settlers thought of the area as their own and over time established a flourishing agricultural-commercial colony. Later, the British came to South Africa, replacing the Dutch colonial administration and forcing the earlier Dutch settlers north into the Transvaal, the Orange Free State, and the heart of Africa. There, rather like in the pre–Civil War South, they lived in isolation, practicing a strict form of Protestantism that consigned Africans to a lower place in the social order.

South Africa became independent in 1911. It was dominated by whites; blacks, working in the mines and fields, lived a separate and lower-class existence, or were outside of the money-market economy entirely. Over time, white rule, now including German, French, British, Portuguese, and other influences as well as the original Dutch, collectively called "Afrikaners," was consolidated, eventually coming together in the apartheid regime. Under apartheid (which means "apart"), whites and blacks lived almost completely separate lives, with the whites enjoying a privileged position and the blacks subjugated. The system was blatantly racist but it also provided for significant economic growth and the modernization of South Africa.

In the 1950s and 1960s, blacks had organized, in the form of the African National Congress (ANC), an armed resistance movement to white rule. Whites had the money, the police, and the armed forces, but blacks outnumbered them by about nine to one. Many were predicting the disintegration of South Africa into chaos and bloody, racial civil war. But cooler heads prevailed on both sides, and in 1994 South Africa held its first election in which blacks were fully enfranchised. The ANC and its leader, the saintly Nelson Mandela, won; civil war was avoided.

South Africa has been governed by the ANC since 1994. Crime is a major problem as is the competence of the government. For whites, who consider themselves South Africans, the issue is whether they should move away from the country they love, or stay in a place where they will now constitute a permanent minority, disadvantaged by the black government's affirmative action programs. It is a tough decision that almost all young whites now face. And if they, with their education levels, skills, and entrepreneurial talents, now leave, can the South African economy continue to thrive? Or will South Africa become "just another" African country, threatening to sink to failed state levels?

The United States has a major stake in South Africa's success. First, the country is enormously rich in natural resources, to say nothing of its strategic location commanding all of southern Africa and its waterways. Second, we *want* South Africa to succeed: if Africa's richest and best-educated state sinks into failure, it will send a depressing message for the rest of Africa. Third, many Americans, black and white, were involved in one way or another in the antiapartheid struggle (which they often saw as like the U.S. civil rights battle); they follow South African events and want fervently for this experiment in black rule to succeed. For these reasons, Americans pay more attention to events in South Africa than to happenings elsewhere on the African continent.

Nigeria

With 140 million people, Nigeria is Africa's most populous country and one of its largest. It is the world's eighth largest oil producer and is rich in other resources as well. A former British colony, Nigeria also has the advantage in today's globalized world of speaking English. When the issue comes up of including a major African state on the UN Security Council, it is usually Nigeria that is mentioned. Nigeria is included as part of an overall UN agreement that would include Brazil in South America, Japan and India in Asia, and Germany in Europe.

While Nigeria holds considerable promise, it is also beset by many problems. Its per capita income of $1,770 places it, despite its oil wealth, among the poorest African countries, in the low-income category. Perhaps because of its oil wealth, it is also one of the most corrupt countries in the world. Nigerians say two things about their oil: first, if we are so rich, why should we work hard?—not a good omen for national development. And second, if we are so rich and yet the people so poor, it must be because of corrupt leaders. In fact, for most of its history, Nigeria has been dominated by leaders who are both corrupt and authoritarian, with most of its leaders coming from military ranks.

Nigeria sits on a line, rather like the Sudan and other Central African countries, that divides northern and Islamic Africa from southern and Christian Africa. That line runs right across the middle of Nigeria and splits the country into religious regions that are frequently at war with one another. The northern states (Nigeria is a federal country) are Muslim and often practice Islamic sharia law, though in a mixed form that blends more easygoing African characteristics. The south is not only Christian, but it is the wealthier and better-educated part of Nigeria and has long dominated the government, the army, the economy, and the bureaucracy. These resentments, coupled with religious hatreds and complicated by ethnic and tribal rivalries, have led to uprisings in the north, attacks by Muslims on their Christian neighbors, and retaliation by Christian communities against the growing and more militant Muslims.

Nigeria, even with all its problems, is an important country and particularly for U.S. policy. First, we would like to see Nigeria's new and still wobbly democracy flourish as a way of stabilizing the country. For the same reason, we want to have corruption curtailed and an honest, efficient, civilian government in power in Lagos, the capital. Obviously, oil and our need for it also figures strongly in our calculations regarding Nigeria. In addition, we see a strong, prosperous, stable, and democratic Nigeria serving as a bulwark against rising Islamic fundamentalism and terrorism spreading from east (Somalia) to west and from north to south in Africa. The stakes here are becoming higher, which is one of the key reasons the United States created a new military command (AFRICOM) for the continent.

Conclusion

The problems of Africa sometimes seem overwhelming. One is tempted—and many Africa observers have done so—to throw up one's hands in despair, to give up on the continent. The problems include extreme poverty, illiteracy, inequities in the international economy, lack of a strong middle class, small markets, corruption, disease, mass starvation, a harsh climate, lack of trained personnel, AIDS, ineffective government, a largely peasant and traditional population, authoritarian regimes, civil war, violence, fear, genocide, tribal and ethnic rivalries, weak civil society, undefined borders, strong or "big" men, and inefficiency. Almost every problem that one can think of afflicting the poor and developing world is present in Africa to an extreme degree.

If the problems are so great and governments so ineffective, the temptation will be strong to give up on the region in a foreign policy sense as well. International relations and foreign policy, after all, are based on a two-way contract: you give me something, I give you something, and we both benefit in the end. However, in Africa the direction seems to be mainly one way: the developed nations provide aid but receive little in return. That is not a good basis for a mutually beneficial policy. If that is an accurate portrayal of Africa's situation, then the quip popular in Washington a few years ago would apply: let the humanitarian relief agencies help Africa with food and other basics, have AFRICOM ready to put out the brush fires and civil wars, and for the rest, stay out.

But such a policy of not-too-benign neglect will not do anymore. First, Africa has shown significant improvement in economic development, democratization, and poverty reduction in recent years. That means we can partner better with the African nations than in the past. Second, Africa has vast and still largely untapped resources that we can use: oil, timber, metals, diamonds, many others. The presence of these resources provides a basis for trade, investment, and business. Third, we need to recognize that other emerging powers—China, India, Brazil, Russia, as well as the larger European countries of France, Germany, Italy, Spain, and Great Britain—are all increasingly active in Africa and are cementing their relations there. The United States need not be in Africa just because these other nations are; rather, we need to be in Africa because it is in *our interests* to be there.

Notes

1. Hereafter referred to simply as Africa. When we say "sub-Saharan Africa," we exclude North Africa—Morocco, Algeria, Libya, Tunisia, and Egypt—which is categorized as part of the Middle East.

2. I am indebted here to my CSIS colleagues Jennifer Cooke and J. Stephen Morrison (eds.), *U.S. Africa Policy beyond the Bush Years: Critical Challenges for the Obama Administration* (Washington, D.C.: CSIS, 2009).

Suggested Readings

Bratton, Michael and Nicolas van de Walle. *Democratic Experiments in Africa* (Cambridge, UK: Cambridge University Press, 1997).

Chazan, Naomi (ed.). *Politics and Society in Contemporary Africa* (Boulder, CO: Lynne Rienner, 1992).

Clark, Leon. *Through African Eyes* (New York: CITE Books, 1991).

Cooke, Jennifer and J. Stephen Morrison (eds.). *U.S. Africa Policy* (Washington, D.C.: Center for Strategic and International Studies, 2009).

Council on Foreign Relations. *More Than Humanitarianism: A Strategic U.S. Approach toward Africa* (New York: Council on Foreign Relations, 2006).

Davidson, Basil. *The Black Man's Burden: Africa and the Curse of the Nation-State* (New York: Times Books, 1992).

Harbeson, J. and D. Rothchild (eds.). *Africa in World Politics* (Boulder, CO: Westview, 1995).

Mazrui, Ali. *The Africans* (London: BBC Publications, 1986).

Ottaway, Marina. *Africa's New Leaders* (Washington, D.C.: Carnegie Endowment, 1999).

Potholan, Christian. *Theory and Practice of African Politics* (Englewood Cliffs, NJ: Prentice Hall, 1973).

Young, Crawford. *The African Colonial State in Comparative Perspective* (New Haven, CT: Yale University Press, 1994).

CHAPTER 9

Conclusion

Theoretical Issues

We started off in this book with two theoretical and methodological issues. I know readers are often bored by theoretical and methodological issues, but unless we get our basic ideas clear, nothing else will make much sense. The first issue was the growing separation between comparative politics as a field of study and international relations/foreign policy as another. The second has to do with the growing emphasis *within* the IR field on quantification, mathematical modeling, and the growing effort aimed to make IR "scientific," often to the exclusion of concern with real-life foreign policy issues, problems, and debates.

Part of the issue has to do with the growing professionalization and, hence, specialization of these respective fields. As the fields of political science, development studies, and international affairs become more professionalized within our nation's colleges and universities, they also become more specialized in their respective subfields. Each field and subfield develops its own literature, language, theory, methodology, gurus, disciples, camp followers, and so on. In the process, these fields grow ever farther apart and with fewer overlaps. It is an old public administration principle: when you separate, in this case by distinct subfields, you really do, in terms of approaches, thinking, and so on, separate.

The growing separation of the fields and subfields creates its own set of problems. One of the problems is that international relations seem to have less and less to say to policymakers. It is more and more isolated within its own narrow research terrain. Of course, this is not true across the board: many colleges and universities continue to offer courses and research analysis, mainly at the undergraduate level, that are eminently practical, down-to-earth, and relevant to foreign policy-making. But at the graduate or professional school level, that is true less and less. That is one of the key reasons why research and advice on foreign policy-making has, over the last thirty years, gravitated away from the nation's colleges and universities and toward more specialized research centers, such as Harvard's Weatherhead Center for International Affairs (WCFIA), and the Washington-based think tanks, such as the Center for Strategic and International Studies (CSIS).[1]

My own view is that these gaps can still be bridged. On the one hand, I am convinced that the subfield of comparative politics has a great deal to offer to the field of international relations and foreign policy. For comparative politics' field of inquiry is *all* of the world's political systems: surely we can agree that, to have an enlightened policy toward a country or region, it helps enormously to have the most detailed and thorough knowledge possible about that country or region presented in an analytic and systematic way. That is what comparative politics can do.

At the same time, while we all want the international relations/foreign policy field to be as professional and scholarly as possible, most of us also want it to be relevant to real-world issues and policies. After all, that is why most of us went into this field: not just to study IR and political science for their own sakes (although that may be important, too), but to utilize our professional and specialized knowledge to help enlighten public policy, including foreign policy. That is, in any case, the orientation on which the present book is based.

Shifting Regional Priorities

We live in momentous times. One of the reasons they are momentous is that America's regional and continental foreign policy priorities are changing, often dramatically. The world's geopolitical fault lines and templates are shifting—and not just geologically but politically and strategically as well. Hence a title for this book might be, "Continental Drift."

Historically, Europe was *the* focus of American foreign policy. That's where most of our forebears came from; we had strong historical and cultural ties to Europe (not least, coming to Europe's defense in World Wars I and II); and the Trans-Atlantic Alliance, in the form of the North American Treaty Organization (NATO), helped preserve the peace during the long Cold War. We also have strong business, commercial, investment, and trade relations with Europe that may prove to be more durable than our security and diplomatic alliance. It may be still that our closest friends and allies—Great Britain, Germany, the Netherlands; we're not too sure about France or Spain—are in Europe.

But now things are changing. Asia is the center of the world's most dynamic economies. It is also the most populous area of the world and with more nuclear powers than any other area. In addition, Europe and the United States have been drifting further apart: we no longer share the same religious, economic, or political values as in the past. So U.S. attention is, quite naturally, shifting away from Europe and toward Asia; that is, as the bank robbers often say, "where the money is."

But we want to do the shift toward Asia in a way that keeps the old European alliance system—still useful even though the Cold War is over—and maintains our friendship with the key European countries. The addition of a host of East European countries to NATO and to the European Union (EU) gives us a number of key allies in that region who may be closer to us politically than some of the Western Europeans, now referred to in some quarters as "old Europe." In addition, our commercial ties with and investments in Europe may trump the cultural and political trends presently pulling the United States and Europe apart. In sum, while U.S. attention begins to concentrate on other areas of the world, we very much want to maintain our ties with Europe.

And then, there is Russia. Is Russia a part of Europe or no? Well, yes and no. First, Russia is a huge country, the world's largest, straddling *both* Asia and Europe and bordering on the Middle East as well (and with large Islamic minorities), so its loyalties and directions are sometimes split. Second, Russia thinks of itself as a separate civilization—"Great Russia." Its literature, culture, and religion (Orthodoxy) make it a distinct region unto itself. Hence, it is not certain that it wants to join Europe or the two great European "clubs," the EU and NATO; nor has it been asked, which adds perversely to the Russian desire not to join. Third, this is an urban-rural split: Moscow and Saint Petersburg are more Western-oriented, while the rest of the country looks inward.

Since the collapse of the Soviet Union in 1991, Russia has shrunk drastically in size, population, and internal coherence. Large parts of the former Soviet Union—the Baltics, Belarus, the Ukraine, Central Asia, Georgia, the Trans-Caucuses—have become independent states; the population of Russia has gone from 300 million to 170 million. In addition, life expectancy in Russia is low; alcoholism and corruption are widespread; and the economy has taken a nosedive. Many parts of Russia are closer to the poor Third World than to the First. On top of this social and economic decline, Russian institutions, including its once-vaunted army and security apparatus, have been gravely weakened.

Should we, therefore, no longer treat Russia as a major power? As a power, yes, especially in its immediate surrounding area; but not as a superpower. Russia is no longer, in its weakened state, a threat to us, but it is to its smaller neighbors. President Vladimir Putin is trying to revive Russian power and make it into a superpower again, but he has a long way to go. Therefore, we need to keep an eye on the Russian "Bear" and keep it from harassing its neighbors; but except in this very limited way, we do not at this stage need to fear the Russians or resurrect the old Cold War containment strategy. Russia is a worry, but it is not a danger. For now, at least, Russia can be downgraded in our list of priorities.

While Europe and Russia are slipping, Asia is clearly rising. It is rising especially in terms of its economic power, but it is also rising in the ranks of U.S. priorities. When we think of Asia these days, we mainly think of China, but remember that Japan is still the third largest economy in the world and South Korea, Taiwan, Hong Kong, Singapore, and now Malaysia and India are economic dynamos as well. In addition, there are five known nuclear powers—Russia, North Korea, China, India, and Pakistan—in Asia, and three others—South Korea, Japan, and Taiwan—that either already have secret nuclear weapons or are so close to having them that they could be developed on short notice.

Asia's rising importance on economic, political, strategic, and diplomatic grounds has forced the United States to reorient its priorities in that direction and to forge new cooperative mutual security agreements with Japan, South Korea, China, and India. Our hearts and our cultural background may still be mainly in Europe, but our pocketbooks and our macro-strategic concerns are now mainly in Asia.

While Asia is of fundamental long-term importance, the issues that mainly preoccupy us on a day-to-day basis are in the Middle East. Think of Iraq, Iran, Afghanistan, and the Israeli-Palestinian conflict—among others! And then recall the quote from a former American secretary of state that he had to *struggle* on a daily basis to keep the Middle East from taking up 100 percent of his time.

All of these Middle East issues are dangerous, violent, and potentially explosive. Moreover, they are fueled by intense hatred and long-standing enmities. Think of the similarly explosive Balkans in southeast Europe, but with far greater dangers and also nuclear weapons thrown in. The Arabs hate the Israelis with a passion; Israelis, in turn, look down on the Arabs as the carriers of an inferior religion and civilization. These are, of course, inflammatory sentiments that could produce violence at almost any time. Then throw in terrorism, nuclear weapons (Israel and the potential of same in Muslim hands), and long-standing blood feuds among rival Middle East groups, and you have a formula for dynamite. Then to this simmering brew, if we add oil and its absolute necessity for the health of the U.S., European, and Asian economies, we have the beginning of an understanding of what makes the Middle East volatile.

In Latin America we have a similar issue. But while in the Middle East the issues are mainly strategic—terrorism, a nuclear Iran, oil, Israel's security—in Latin America the issues are mainly social, political, cultural, and economic. While the Middle East has the potential to take up 100 percent of the secretary of state's time, Latin America has the potential to take up 100 percent or nearly so of the time of our *civilian* agencies, especially those dealing with drugs, immigration, housing, education, welfare, trade, tourism, investment—the list goes on. Because, while other areas of the world are more important to the United States in a strategic sense, no other area of the world has more capacity to affect us domestically than does Latin America.

There are only a handful of issues emanating from Latin America that affect us *strategically*. A failed and destabilized state in Mexico that sends *millions* of its citizens streaming toward the U.S. border, drug gangs that seize control of parts or all of the Colombian or Mexican states, or terrorists entering the United States along our southern (including the Caribbean) border—these are among the security issues that we need to worry about in Latin America. And since we share the Western Hemisphere with Latin America and have some elements of a common Western heritage, we need also to work for democracy and human rights in the area.

But our main concern, since we are interdependent with Latin America on so many issues, is the immense impact, mainly through immigration, that Latin America has on U.S. *society*. This may not be a strategic issue, but it certainly is a large social, political, economic, and cultural one. We are becoming, in some regions, an Hispanic country; certainly, Hispanics are now the country's largest minority. These facts present a host of issues for us domestically; they raise Latin America in terms of its importance to us; and they dictate that the United States should have good, normal, and mature relations with its neighbors to the south.

Africa is another of those areas, like Latin America, that is or should be of rising importance to us. For a long time the United States largely ignored Africa, leaving it to the former colonial powers of France, Great Britain, and Portugal to police, when needed, their ex-colonies. But now that is changing: the former colonial powers cannot or will not do the "policing" or "fire-fighting" functions anymore, and we are discovering that Africa has importance to us after all.

For one thing, African-Americans are increasingly interested in the continent of their origins; for another, we have discovered that Africa has vast resources—timber, oil, precious metals, gems, gold, agricultural products—that we can certainly use. In addition, we have realized that if we don't exploit these resources, China and India certainly will; we have also discovered that failed states in Africa, such as Somalia, serve as terrorist breeding grounds for persons and groups intent on attacking the United States. Hence, we have created AFRICOM, the African military defense command, and our civilian agencies and nongovernmental organizations (NGOs) are expanding their interest in Africa as well. Rather like Latin America, except that it is farther away and does not affect us so directly, Africa is clearly a continent of rising importance in U.S. strategic and political consideration.

* * *

The argument presented here can be summarized in the following ways. First, the relative importance of all these distinct world regions is shifting. In the large, geopolitical scheme of things, both Europe and Russia have lost importance. They are still important to us in many ways and we want to maintain good and constructive relations with them, but *relative* to other areas, both Europe and Russia are less important to us now than they were twenty years ago.

At the same time, other areas are rising in importance. These include, most importantly, Asia and the Middle East. The reasons for Asia's importance should be self-evident: dynamic economies, a changed global center of gravity that points toward it, large populations, and nuclear weapons. Asia is now emerging as number one in U.S. priorities, although some scholars would, for historical and alliance reasons, still rank Europe on a par with Asia. The latter interpretation is borne out by our own computation, which shows Europe and Asia tied in terms of importance (see table 9.1).

The Middle East also ranks high and is rising in importance. Here the issues are not just Iranian nukes, terrorism, and wars in Iraq

Table 9.1   Criteria of importance by region

Country/region	Total points	Political	Economic	Social	Strategic	Cultural	Democracy/human rights
Europe	(15)	High	High	High	Medium	High	Low
Russia	(9)	Medium	Low	Low	Medium	Low	Medium
Asia	(15)	High	High	Medium	High	Medium	Medium
Middle East	(13)	High	High	Low	High	Low	Low
Latin America	(12)	Low	High	Medium	Medium	Medium	Medium
Africa	(5)	Low	Medium	Low	Medium	Low	Low

and Afghanistan, but also and longer term, oil, Israel, and overall security.

Latin America is also a rising and upcoming area in terms of its importance to the United States, as is Africa. Though both are rising on our scale, Latin America, mainly for economic, social, and cultural reasons, is rising faster and occupies a higher position than does Africa. I think we should see these two areas as providing opportunities for the United States and for an opportunity-based foreign policy, as compared with the threat-based foreign policy present in other areas.

Overall, what we see are two areas—Europe and Russia—declining in overall importance, and four areas—Asia, the Middle East, Latin America, and Africa—rising in importance. However, some of these areas, Asia, for example, are rising faster and in terms of a larger number of criteria than others. In addition, one could argue that, since the volatile Middle East has the capability/possibility, at present, of unleashing a more general global confrontation, there the strategic variable should receive greater weight than the others.

The End of an Era?

From this discussion, it is clear that there are many foreign policy issues for the United States to grapple with. Four points in conclusion need to be raised.

First, do we have so many issues on our foreign policy plate that we cannot handle them all? Is "the system" so overloaded that it cannot cope? Here I am reminded of former secretary of state Colin Powell's quip that every morning, when he got up, he already had forty-seven problems accumulated overnight on his plate to deal with. The last thing he needed as he went through his day, he said, was for anyone or any one country to add number forty-eight to the list! Put another way, given all the problems and uncertainties "out there" in the world, can the United States continue to be the world's policeman and fireman, solving problems and putting out brush fires wherever they occur? Or have we reached a stage of what we might call policeman's or fireman's fatigue: too many problems, too few resources, so let someone else deal with them for a change?

Which gets us to the second issue. Can we afford it? Can we afford to continue our role as global policeman, fireman, and peacemaker? The answer is, probably not. The United States is, at this stage, essentially bankrupt. We are deeply in debt to other countries, chiefly China. Our industrial and manufacturing base can no longer compete globally and is shutting down. Unemployment is rising to unprecedented levels. We are printing untold trillions of paper money without much in the way of hard securities or resources to back it up. The United States is living way beyond its means, a debtor nation, sacrificing the needs of future generations to our own demands for an extravagant lifestyle that we can no longer afford. So where will the money come from for us to be a global peacemaker? Eventually, and probably sooner rather than later, reality will set in. Over time we will have to do the strict cost-benefit analysis that was never done for Iraq, Afghanistan, or the war on terrorism: exactly how much will this cost, where will the money come from, how much exactly are we getting in return for our money, and what is our exit strategy?

A third and related issue is U.S. domestic weakness. We are a deeply divided nation.[2] Public opinion is deeply divided; our historic political culture is fraying and fragmenting; our political parties are not only poles apart ideologically but the partisan debate is increasingly nasty and mean-spirited as well. Interest group politics tends to polarize every issue; within the government, what we call "bureaucratic politics" (turf and budgetary rivalries between agencies) hinders us from carrying out effective policy. Our media and think tanks reinforce and perpetuate these deep political and policy divisions; both Congress and the White House are more and more dysfunctional. Given all these divisions and dysfunctions that seem only to be getting deeper, how can we carry out an effective global foreign policy? The answer is that we can't. For in a democracy, if the country is deeply divided, ultimately policymaking will be conflictual and unsuccessful as well.

Meanwhile, fourth, as the United States has grown weaker, other countries and regions have grown stronger. Think of China, Germany, Japan, India, Brazil, and now a nuclear Iran. Almost all of these, reflecting their newfound influence, are slated fairly soon for membership on the UN Security Council. Our traditional allies, Great Britain and France, are weaker presently than previously, but they still carry considerable weight and now, with a unified Europe in the form of the European Union, with its own foreign and defense policy, maybe Europe will make a strategic comeback. Then, too, while Russia is down now, who doubts that over time Russia will recover and resume its role as a major power?

The upshot is that the United States is no longer the only power in the world. And our weaknesses as outlined earlier encourage other rising countries to fill the vacuum. Look at the list in the preceding paragraph: there are at least eight or nine rising new, or old, powers, in addition to the United States itself. And let us not forget other actual or potential dynamos such as South Korea (or perhaps one day a unified Korea), Israel, Egypt, Turkey, Nigeria, South Africa, Indonesia, Pakistan, and Mexico. All of these are large and significant countries; all have the potential to be at least regional powers; and quite a few of them can cause immense trouble in the world. The point is that the United States is no longer alone as a superpower; there are other rising powers out there ready to challenge us; and increasingly, we will be forced to act in concert with these other countries and no longer alone or unilaterally.

Adding these factors up, it is clear that U.S. foreign policy is facing a crisis of multiple dimensions. On the one hand, we are *relatively* weaker, economically and politically, than we used to be. On the other, other countries and regions are rising up to challenge us, and may have already arrived! At the same time, there are more and more crises with which to contend: within nations, between nations, within and between various culture or geographic areas such as Asia, the West, or the Middle East (think of Samuel Huntington's "Clash of Civilizations"), and on a global basis (climate change, acid rain, and the like). Meanwhile, there appears to be a seemingly growing incapacity on the part of the United States itself, and in terms of our ability and willingness to try to solve these problems.

When I was in college, my friends and I had an expression that we used frequently. Romances, grades, our college football team were all, at one time or another, "going to hell in a hand basket." I haven't heard that expression in a while; and even at the time we used it, I don't believe any of us truly believed it. It was only an expression, a gross exaggeration. For that was an optimistic time in America, a time of John F. Kennedy, the Peace Corps, the Great Society. We were going to "go any distance, pay any price, solve any problem," and eliminate poverty, racism, and underdevelopment, all at the same time.

Today, we are not so optimistic or so hopeful. We have been chastised. We recognize limits; if we do not, we had better! But that does not mean such unalloyed pessimism as expressed earlier. The world is probably *not* "going to hell in a hand basket," although it may at times seem that way. We need to adjust to new realities. It *is* a new world out there. Today it's much harder for us to go it alone in the world. It's harder to influence other countries. We need allies; we need to build consensus; we need to work more closely with and through international organizations. We need a little more humility, much greater understanding of other peoples and cultures, less certainty that we know all the answers. We need to reinvigorate our economy and get our budget deficits under control.

The world can still be a wonderful place. But it is much more complicated and difficult than it used to be, and our own power and influence are more limited. Complexity does not necessarily mean despair, however. But it does mean we need to redouble our efforts, both domestically and in terms of all those other fascinating countries, regions, and cultures that are the subject of this book, to understand them better, and to devise appropriate strategies and policies for them.

Notes

1. I have been working on a series of books detailing the transfer of policy influence from the nation's universities to the Washington-based think tanks and policy shops. See Howard J. Wiarda, *Universities, Think Tanks, and War Colleges* (Princeton, NJ: XLibris, 1999); Wiarda, *Conservative Braintrust: The Rise, Fall, and Rise Again of the American Enterprise Institute* (Lanham, MD: Lexington Press, 2009); Wiarda, *Harvard and the Weatherhead Center for International Affairs: Think Tank, Research Center, and Incubator of Presidents* (Lexington, forthcoming); Wiarda, *Think Tanks and Foreign Policy: The Foreign Policy Research Institute and Presidential Politics* (Lexington, forthcoming); Wiarda, *Universities in Decline: From the Great Society to Today—How Universities Have Been Replaced by Washington Think Tanks as the Generators of Policy Ideas* (forthcoming); and Wiarda, *A Clash of Cultures: Military Brass vs. Academics at the National War College* (forthcoming).

2. For a complementary book to the present volume, which focuses not on foreign countries or regions, but on the domestic bases of U.S. foreign policy, see Howard J. Wiarda, *Divided America on the World Stage: Broken Government and Foreign Policy* (Washington, D.C.: Potomac Publishers, 2009).

Suggested Readings

Fukuyama, Francis. *America At the Crossroads* (New Haven, CT: Yale University Press, 2006).

Ghani, Ashraf and Clare Lockhart. *Fixing Failed States* (New York: Oxford University Press, 2008).

Hansen, Carol Rae (ed.). *The New World Order: Rethinking America's Global Role* (Flagstaff, AZ: Arizona Honors Academy Press, 1992).

Ikenberry, G. John et al. *The Crisis of American Foreign Policy* (Princeton, NJ: Princeton University Press, 2009).

Johnson, Haynes and David S. Broder. *The System: The American Way of Politics at the Breaking Point* (Boston: Little Brown, 1996).

Lake, Anthony et al. *Our Own Worst Enemy: The Unmaking of Americas Foreign Policy* (New York: Simon and Schuster, 1985).

Magstadt, Thomas M. *Nations and Governments: Comparative Politics in Regional Perspective* (New York: St. Martin's Press, 1994).

Nye, Joseph F., Jr. *The Paradox of American Power* (New York: Oxford University Press, 2002).

Rosati, Jerel. *The Politics of United States Foreign Policy* (Belmont, CA: Wadsworth/Thomson, 2006).

Spanier, John and Eric Uslaner. *American Foreign Policy and the Democratic Dilemma* (New York: Macmillan, 1994).

Wiarda, Howard J. *Divided America on the World Stage: Broken Government and Foreign Policy* (Washington, D.C.: Potomac Publishers, 2009).

Zakaria, Fareed. *The Post-American World* (New York: Norton, 2008).

Index